BETH FELKER JONES

WHY I AM

PROTESTANT

ivp
Academic

An imprint of InterVarsity Press
Downers Grove, Illinois

InterVarsity Press
P.O. Box 1400 | Downers Grove, IL 60515-1426
ivpress.com | email@ivpress.com

InterVarsity Press® is the publishing division of InterVarsity Christian Fellowship/USA®. For more information, visit intervarsity.org.

Scripture quotations, unless otherwise noted, are from the New Revised Standard Version, Updated Edition. Copyright © 2021 National Council of Churches of Christ in the United States of America. Used by permission. All rights reserved worldwide.

The publisher cannot verify the accuracy or functionality of website URLs used in this book beyond the date of publication.

Cover design: David Fassett
Interior design: Daniel van Loon

ISBN 978-1-5140-0300-8 (print) | ISBN 978-1-5140-0301-5 (digital)

Printed in the United States of America ♾

Library of Congress Cataloging-in-Publication Data
Names: Jones, Beth Felker, 1976- author
Title: Why I am Protestant / Beth Felker Jones.
Description: Downers Grove, IL : IVP Academic, [2025] | Series: Ecumenical
  dialogue series | Includes bibliographical references and index.
Identifiers: LCCN 2025007610 (print) | LCCN 2025007611 (ebook) | ISBN
  9781514003008 paperback | ISBN 9781514003015 ebook
Subjects: LCSH: Protestantism–Apologetic works
Classification: LCC BX4811.3 .J66 2025 (print) | LCC BX4811.3 (ebook) |
  DDC 280/.4–dc23/eng/20250516
LC record available at https://lccn.loc.gov/2025007610
LC ebook record available at https://lccn.loc.gov/2025007611

32   31   30   29   28   27   26   25 | 13   12   11   10   9   8   7   6   5   4   3   2   1

"*Why I Am Protestant* provides a succinct but thorough account of Protestant Christianity, elevating Protestant gifts while valuing Christian unity. Beth Felker Jones writes with characteristic sincerity, charity, and creativity. This is a gift for students, pastors, and all Christians seeking to better understand their own theological inheritance."

Kaitlyn Schiess, senior editor at Holy Post Media and author of *The Ballot and the Bible*

"Beth Felker Jones is one of the most important theologians writing today. Whatever your Christian tradition happens to be, her clear, wise, lyrical voice in *Why I Am Protestant* will feed your soul. Take and read."

Timothy Larsen, Carolyn and Fred McManis Professor of Christian Thought and professor of history at Wheaton College

"In recent years, we have seen significant numbers of erstwhile Protestants swimming the Tiber to become Roman Catholics. This trend has sparked all kinds of soul-searching among the heirs of the Reformation. What are we to make of this? Is our faith sturdy enough to withstand honest questioning? Are the bold claims of Rome true after all? In her new book, which is part autobiography and part historical theology, Beth Felker Jones provides a welcome apologia for Protestant belief."

Chris Castaldo, lead pastor of New Covenant Church of Naperville and author of *Talking with Catholics about the Gospel: A Guide for Evangelicals*

"This kind of book could easily be polemical—'I'm right, you're wrong, let's fight.' Thankfully, Beth Felker Jones takes the higher way of offering a thoughtful, personal, and gracious invitation to Protestantism. Summarizing Protestant thought and spirituality is extremely difficult, and Jones presents a winsome and compelling summary. Here is a key takeaway from the book: Jones identifies how Protestantism helps me to see Christ more clearly, love Christ more dearly, and follow Christ more nearly, day by day. I learned a lot—about myself!—from this book."

Nijay K. Gupta, professor of New Testament at Northern Seminary

"My work has propelled me to engage with Catholic and Orthodox theology and so, also, to provide an answer for why I remain Protestant. Beth Felker Jones provides the reasoning and the words to give voice to my inarticulate senses. A perfect blend of her scholarly expertise and flair for warm and playfully stimulating prose, *Why I Am Protestant*, is for all Christians to appreciate the faith communities that have raised us and with whom we continue to journey. It is especially beneficial for Protestants, a gracious and honest, yet also bold, defense of our contributions to the unity of the body of Christ."

Amy Peeler, Kenneth T. Wessner Chair of Biblical Studies at Wheaton College and author of *Women and the Gender of God* and *Hebrews: Commentary for Christian Formation*

"Beth Felker Jones is one of the most valued and trusted theologians of our day. In *Why I Am Protestant*, she pulls back the curtain to reveal the way in which her convictions as a follower of Christ and expert in theology meet her commitment to the Protestant tradition. What follows is written with her characteristic clarity, insight, and skill as she explores the particular faithfulness of the Protestant tradition as well as its bond to the global Christian faith. Highly recommend!"

Jennifer Powell McNutt, Franklin S. Dyrness Professor of Biblical and Theological Studies at the Litfin Divinity School at Wheaton College and author of *The Mary We Forgot*

This book is dedicated to my parents—

DEAN AND JOANN,

who raised me Methodist and are now Roman

Catholic, with whom I am grateful to remain one,

in the one body of Christ our Lord

To be true to its own idea, a Reformation must hold its course midway, or through the deep rather, between two extremes. In opposition on the one side to Revolution . . . it must attach itself organically to what is already at hand . . . in regular living union with its previous development. In opposition to simple Restoration . . . or a mere repetition of the old, it must produce from the womb of this the birth of something new.

Philip Schaff, The Principle of Protestantism

You can't actually steal food from a church supper.

Marilynne Robinson, Jack

CONTENTS

Acknowledgments | *ix*

Greeting | *1*

||||||||||||||||||||||||||||||||||||
ONE
Why I Am a Christian | *5*

||||||||||||||||||||||||||||||||||||
TWO
Why I Am Particularly Protestant | *20*

||||||||||||||||||||||||||||||||||||
THREE
How Protestantism Helps Me Be Christian | *36*

||||||||||||||||||||||||||||||||||||
FOUR
Doing Church | *54*

||||||||||||||||||||||||||||||||||||
FIVE
The Difficulties of Protestantism | *73*

||||||||||||||||||||||||||||||||||||
SIX
The Peculiar Strengths of Protestantism | *100*

||||||||||||||||||||||||||||||||||||
SEVEN
Hopes for Christian Unity in Diversity | *115*

||||||||||||||||||||||||||||||||||||
EIGHT
Scripture Passages for Protestants | *125*

Epilogue | *139*

General Index | *143*

Scripture Index | *145*

ACKNOWLEDGMENTS

I'VE WANTED TO WRITE THIS BOOK for a long time. Many thanks to David McNutt for giving me the opportunity to do so.

No book goes into the world without an attendant debt of gratitude. I'm grateful to the people and communities who've supported my writing. Thanks to the saints of VTS, Colton Bernasol, Zach Gordon, and the team at InterVarsity Press, and my colleagues at Northern Seminary—especially, through a troubled time—president Karen Walker Freeburg and academic dean Mark Quanstrom. Thanks to my research assistants, Kelly Dippolito, Abby Anderson, and Karen Chacko, for editing work and encouragement. Thanks to friends and family, including for listening to my writing complaints. Big old thanks are due, always, to my husband, Brian Jones.

I owe love and thanks to the United Methodist Church: that broken, and then more broken—but nonetheless graced—mess, where I was baptized and I continue to be fed. Thanks to the congregation of Gary United Methodist Church, where I'm loved. Love and thanks too, to my friends who've decided to leave the United Methodist Church, because none of this is easy, and there's no such thing as the church that gets it right.

Thanks to so many mentors and teachers, including the late David Steinmetz, who gifted me with Augustine, Luther, and Wesley and thus with the beauties of Protestantism. Thanks to my Roman Catholic loved ones—including Reinhard, Holly, Edwin, and my parents—to whom I've hoped to remain accountable as I've written this Protestant book. Edwin, no doubt, will let me know where I've failed, and I'm grateful.

GREETING

As a teacher at a Protestant seminary, I want students to understand our institutional location, including understanding something of the unity of and differences between the great Christian traditions. I sometimes tell students I find myself in something of a quandary when I teach about Protestant–Roman Catholic differences (in our Western context, students are usually more aware of and interested in Roman Catholicism than they are in Eastern Orthodoxy, but we do talk about Orthodoxy as well). I tell my students I am trying to navigate a way between two false positions.

On one side, some of my Protestant students have been taught that Roman Catholicism is sub-Christian. They've been told that Roman Catholics don't care about Scripture or that they are not "saved." They believe false stereotypes about Roman Catholicism, or they are not aware of the many ways Catholicism has changed since the sixteenth century. They have not learned to recognize Roman Catholics as fellow Christians who share with Protestants the most central teachings of the Christian faith. I tell them I cannot let this stand.

On the other side, some strands of contemporary North American Christianity are deep in habits of falsely homogenizing that which is in fact diverse. Those habits will not admit any recognition of real and important differences between Christian traditions. This results in pretending all churches are the same, as though belonging to and living with and from a certain Christian tradition does not matter. Against this, I believe those churches and traditions are best honored with clarity about differences and identities, and as a Christian of Protestant conviction, I'm persuaded there are very good reasons for affirming particularly Protestant faith.

I want to be charitable to Christian traditions other than my own. I want to recognize our shared riches in Christ. I also want to be honest about intra-Christian differences and clear about Protestant conviction. I will not navigate this perfectly, and so I may sometimes seem either too soft or too hard on other traditions. None of us is faultless in attempting clarity and charity, and we all narrate things in ways colored by our judgments and experiences.

It's also the case that Christian traditions—including Protestantism, Roman Catholicism, and Eastern Orthodoxy—can be narrated in various ways. We can speak of the best (or the worst) of official doctrine; we can speak of interpretation of that doctrine as it is practiced in life on the ground in the church; we can speak historically; and we can speak locally. We can speak optimistically, attending to ideal accounts; and we can speak pessimistically, zeroing in on the worst instantiations of church practice. My narration of Protestant conviction does not try to neatly sort these ways of speaking, one from another, because I believe that is how actual belief and practice work. We may attend to the official, but we will always be formed by lived faith. It may be true that "*x* isn't the best official account of *y*" while also being true that "*x* is widely believed or practiced in *y* tradition." This book doesn't provide a comprehensive account of Protestantism, whether historically, theologically, or globally. It doesn't claim to provide *the* right account of Protestant history or theology. It simply narrates my own way of sorting through some key theological matters of Protestant Christian faith and life. I hope this book, along with the others in this series, will help you to think faithfully about the unity and diversity of the one church of Jesus Christ.

ONE

||||||||||||||||||||||||||||

WHY I AM A CHRISTIAN

CHRISTIAN FAITH IS MY LIFE, my center, my every-thing. Jesus Christ is the one who animates my days, who gives me purpose and pulls me through, and who has shaped me, in big and small ways, for as long as I can remember. This is true professionally. My work is to teach and write about Christian theology, but it's also true in every aspect of my life.

This makes the task of writing about why I am a Christian feel quite weighty. The personal stakes are high. What if I can't articulate my answer well enough? (I won't; there's no "enough" to describe Jesus.) What if what I write is unpersuasive? (It cannot be, for it is the Spirit who persuades.) What if I don't have anything new to say? (I won't; I'm speaking of a faith with a long history and of a God who does not change.)

The parentheticals are my courage to keep writing. I don't expect to offer an account of my faith that somehow surpasses other accounts. While I have personal things to say, I won't have anything radically new to say, because who Jesus is and what he has done are not new. I write, then, vulnerably, to place my story in the context of my larger narrative in this book. I write to help you, my reader, understand why I am Protestant.

This chapter locates Protestant faith in its context: the context of the Christian faith as a whole. Protestant faith is first and foremost Christian faith, and the Protestant distinctives I'll spend much of this book talking about matter far less than does that shared faith. The shared faith of Christians across traditions—including Eastern Orthodox, Roman Catholic, and Protestant—is far and away more significant than the matters separating those traditions. I remain convinced that Christians across traditions share the deposit of faith, which fits the rule of Vincent of Lerins; we believe that which Christians "everywhere, always, and all" (*ubique, semper et ab omnibus*) have embraced.[1] If I can't make that clear here, at the outset, I don't want to write the rest of this book, because I'll be talking about secondary matters split off from what comes first. In this chapter, I speak of why I am Christian in three ways. First, I'll talk about my own story, then I'll step back to talk about the big picture of Christian faith, and finally, I'll ask us to think about what it means that God is the good God of good news.

A LIFE

I could start by saying I-grew-up-in-a-Christian-home (uttered quickly, almost all-one-word). Many Christians who, like me,

---

[1]"In the Catholic Church itself, every care should be taken to hold fast to what has been believed everywhere, always, and by all. This is truly and properly 'Catholic,' as indicated by the force and etymology of the name itself, which comprises everything truly universal." Vincent of Lerins, "The Commonitories," in *Writings; Commonitories; Grace and Free Will*, trans. Gerald G. Walsh, Bernard M. Peebles, Rudolph E. Morris, and J. Reginald O'Donnell (Washington, DC: Catholic University of America Press, 1949), 270. For Roman Catholic reflection thereon, see Michael Seewald, *Theories of Doctrinal Development in the Catholic Church*, trans. David West (Cambridge: Cambridge University Press, 2023), 3.3.1.

don't have dramatic conversion stories use this formula to begin to narrate the work of God in their lives. In many Protestant circles, "I-grew-up-in-a-Christian-home" tends to be voiced as an apology, with sheepishness, as though the work of God were less than when it happens through childhood and home and being raised in the church.

Grace, though, works in domesticity and in community. Grace works in parents who nudge their kids out of bed every Sunday, despite the "I don't wanna go" and the "Church is boring." It works in mothers who teach the Lord's Prayer by bedsides and fathers who model giving and integrity. It works in local churches through Sunday school classes and youth groups and sermons and Bible studies. God does not eschew the domestic or the local. God does not disdain the quiet or the small.

God came to us to grow-up-in-a-Jewish-home, and that same God is happy to work in gentle and slow stories in other homes where God is honored. God also works in explosive and public ways. I love the dramatic conversion stories some of my friends can tell. But I am not a Christian because of my quiet story, and those friends aren't Christians because they met God in fire-works. We are Christians because of God. We are Christians because of who God is and what God is doing in our lives, in the church, and in all creation.

My personal narrative, if recounted as a timeline of life events, is a common one. In my Christian home and my local church, I was always looking for and meeting Jesus. I always wanted God. I sang my heart out with the taped praise songs we kept in our car. I made big plans for Bible reading, which I some-times kept, and I prayed earnestly, if sporadically, on retreats and at bedtimes. I resisted the kind of "getting saved" that involves responding to an altar call, partly because my parents had communicated their own distrust of accounts of God's work that would disdain the small and slow and domestic, and partly because it felt disingenuous to make a decision for Jesus when I'd been wanting him for as long as I could recall.

Still, multiple times in multiple years at church camp I raised my hand when it was time to make that decision, checking off the box just in case I needed to do so to formalize Jesus' presence in my life but also confirming and reaffirming my relationship with him. I've learned about Jesus by loving him, by teaching about him—from first efforts as a kindergarten Sunday school teacher and church camp counselor to my present job as a professor of theology—and in the experience of being sustained by him, through the power of the Spirit, through the good and the bad of an ordinary life.

I've known God as I've been fed at the Lord's table, both when my hunger was met by weekly Communion and, during the Covid pandemic, through a long year of fasting. I've known God in weeping over injustice and in discovering God's heart for justice and righteousness. I've known God in the mainline, Methodist church where I was baptized, in the kind of churches that claim nondenominationalism with praise bands and raised hands, in churches with haunting liturgies born in the English Reformation, and in churches in Kenya and Ethiopia where the singing lasts for hours and the many-tongued prayers go on even longer.

All that teaching about Jesus led to a sense that God was calling me, and I went to seminary, where the fuller riches of Christian doctrine and Christian tradition unfolded for me in new ways. I was in love with the same God of my Christian home, whom I was now discovering as the God of Augustine and Aquinas and Julian and Luther, the God of Africa and Asia and my own Midwestern United States, the God of the ancient church and of the Middle Ages, of the Reformation and of the present. I've known God intimately, palpably, as mystic fire, and I've known God when I haven't felt an inkling of the divine presence for years on end.

But the God who was with me from the beginning was constant. My story isn't dramatic, but God's work is. God has transferred me from the dominion of sin and death into the kingdom of holiness and life. God has cleansed my sin and made me new creation, bringing me into right relationship with the Creator. God has knit me together with the body of Christ and given me good work to do as a part of the body. God is changing my life so that I am becoming, with time, more and more like Jesus. I know that's an audacious sentence. God is audacious.

There are no public miracles to show here, but there are countless quiet ones, and that work of God matters to my family and my students. It matters to me. In God's providence, it matters to all creation and to the kingdom that is without end. God is the drama of my story. It's about what God has done, the same thing God has done in countless Christian lives and local churches through the centuries, justifying and sanctifying God's people for life in right relationship to God, each other, and all of creation.

THE BEAUTY OF THE SHARED CHRISTIAN FAITH

I am a Christian because of who God is, and Christian faith acknowledges a God who is more beautiful and more compelling than any human mind could have conceived. We can know this God because of God's goodness in revealing truth about the divine character and nature. The core teachings of the Christian faith are about who God is; and who God is, is why I am a Christian. There are different ways to describe those core teachings; here I'll briefly speak of two. God is the God recognized in the reading of Scripture solidified in the early ecumenical councils, especially Nicaea and Chalcedon. And God is the God of the gospel, the good news for all people announced to the shepherds in Bethlehem and continuing to be announced by Christians today.

The "early ecumenical councils" may sound like a stodgy phrase for the beauty of God, but it points us to the history and the unity of Christian faith. Protestant, Roman Catholic, and Eastern Orthodox Christians all recognize the teaching of these councils.[2] They are "early" because they predate some of the rifts that would give us those groups we now call Protestant, Roman Catholic, and Eastern Orthodox, and they are "ecumenical" because they belong to and are shared by the whole church of God. When we speak, then, of these councils, we are speaking of a great treasure, a deposit of faith that shapes Christians beyond any lines that divide us. We live in a time when many claim that there is nothing that unites Christians across those lines, but scores of worshipers who know God—God as the God of the early ecumenical councils, God as the God revealed in Scripture, the triune God—testify otherwise.

Above I referred to the teaching of these councils as "the reading of Scripture" solidified there. Describing things this

---

[2]Young Richard Kim, *The Cambridge Companion to the Council of Nicaea* (Cambridge: Cambridge University Press, 2021).

way is somewhat Protestant, but you already knew that about me. The early ecumenical councils did not invent their teachings about God. They came to those teachings through sustained and careful wrestling with the Scriptures as the revealed Word of God. The doctrines of the Trinity (Council of Nicaea) and of the person of Christ (Council of Chalcedon) are the best readings of Scripture we have. Unlike other readings (many of which were condemned by these councils as heresies, which are obstinately false teachings about God), the Nicene and Chalcedonian readings of Scripture take up the fullness of the mysteries of the Scriptures, both Old and New Testaments. They do not rely on a few prooftexts. They read the whole story of God's work in the world and help us to describe the God we meet through that story. They show us the God of the Bible, one triune God, the Father who sends the Son to invite us to unity with God through the Spirit.

As a Christian theologian, there is nothing I find more beautiful than this truth. God is God alone, the only God, who reveals the lies of the false gods and the not gods. God is one. God is Father, Son, and Holy Spirit, three persons and still one God, an eternally existing relationship of love, a dynamic of unity and difference. The Father is not some mythic Zeus-type god, not a nationalist muscle man in the sky. The Father is the Father of our Lord Jesus Christ, who reveals the truth about God in his flesh and through his Spirit. Jesus is fully God and fully human. He is the eternal divine Son, sharing his divinity with his Father and Spirit, and he is truly one of us, body and soul. He is truly with us and for us. In this space between Jesus' first coming and the time when he will return in glory, we are not left alone. God the Spirit is with us, indwelling, empowering, and making us holy.

The early ecumenical councils refuted those who would teach otherwise, those who would give a truncated picture of God. Those councils started with the great truth of God's oneness, as revealed to Israel, and they worked to understand how that oneness could fit with the threeness that had now been revealed in the events of the New Testament as the Father sent the Son in the Spirit to be born, live, die, and be raised from the dead for our sake.

The obvious thing to do was to declare that this simply couldn't all fit together. If God is one, God could not be three, so Jesus and the Spirit must be less than God. The school of thought called Arianism taught that the oneness of God was such that it could not be shared, giving us a false god who would need to hoard power to himself to be who he is.[3] Arianism gave us a false Son who was not truly God but a superlative creature, a helper, a second to the Father. This was certainly a neat solution to the question of how oneness might fit with threeness, but it could not account for the full biblical witness to the person of Jesus, for the gracious facts that Jesus does what *only God can do*, that Jesus is Lord and Savior, to be worshiped together with the Father and the Spirit.

Contrary to Arianism, the Council of Nicaea gave us something less neat and more astounding, more beautiful, and more biblical, and that response has rightly been recognized as the truth of Christian faith—as orthodoxy, if you will—for the seventeen hundred years since. Nicaea confirmed that, contrary to expectation, Jesus and the Spirit are both truly and fully God

---

[3]Michael Thompson, "Arianism: Is Jesus Christ Divine and Eternal or Was He Created?," in *Heresies and How to Avoid Them: Why It Matters What Christians Believe*, ed. Ben Quash and Michael Ward (repr., Grand Rapids, MI: Baker Academic, 2007).

(Jn 1:1; 14:5-11; 20:31). Jesus is of one being with the Father (Jn 17:22). The Spirit is the Lord and the giver of life (Rom 8:9-11; 2 Cor 3:17-18). These three are one. The Arian Jesus could not save, for God alone can save. The Arian Spirit, another creature, could not be the truth of God's presence with us, for Arianism made the Spirit less than God. Nicaea rejects the subordinationism of Arianism (putting Jesus and the Spirit underneath the Father), that is, it rejects the assumption that divine power means hierarchy and hoarding. The biblical, Nicene faith gives us the mystery of the Trinity. Three divine persons, coequal and comajestic. The Father is known truly through the Son and the Spirit, the Son speaks with the Father through the Spirit, the Spirit works nothing less than the power of God.

The Council of Chalcedon also wrestled with what seemed like a basic logical problem. How could Jesus, who is truly God, also be human? The obvious answer to the question was that surely, he couldn't be. How could the eternal enter time? The infinite take on the limits of flesh? The Holy One come into this world of sin? Surely the thing must have been just a trick of the light, and Jesus only seemed to be human? Or maybe he was a little bit human but not truly and fully so? Or maybe divinity had swallowed up and overcome whatever was once human about him? (All these ideas were suggested at the time and re-jected at Chalcedon.)[4]

But if Jesus isn't truly and fully human, we are no longer talking about the Jesus revealed in Scripture. We are no longer talking about the Jesus who truly came among us to be *with* us

---

[4]For more on christological heresies, see Frances M. Young, *From Nicaea to Chalcedon: A Guide to the Literature and Its Background* (Grand Rapids, MI: Baker Academic, 2010).

and *for* us, to know our grief, bear our sorrow, empathize with our weakness (Heb 4:14-16). We are no longer talking about the Jesus who was born and grew up, who ate and slept, wept and died (Mt 1:23-25; Mk 15:34-37; Lk 8:22-24; Jn 11:35). A less-than-human Jesus could not draw our humanity into union with his to share a resurrection like his (1 Cor 15). What surprise would it be if a God were raised from the dead? What miracle if the eternal one proved not to have been beaten by death? The mercy, the majesty, and the good news of Jesus' resurrection are that it is the resurrection of one of us mortals, one who, like us, is human, who represents us and promises to bring us, his fellow humans, along the road that he has trod.

Chalcedon affirmed the full divinity and, at the same time, the full humanity of Jesus.[5] The truth about Jesus is that of divinity and humanity (two natures) in one person. He is truly God and truly human. Assuming Jesus to be less than human would have been easier, but it couldn't account for the fullness of the biblical witness to who Jesus is and what he has done, and it would rob of us the beauty and goodness of the God who chose to become one of us, for love of us. The incarnation of the Son is not a party trick. It is the very truth of God with us and for us.

All of this is the shared faith of Eastern Orthodox, Roman Catholic, and Protestant Christians. We worship the same God. We are loved by the same Father, redeemed by the same Son, indwelt by the same Spirit. This account of who God is comes with an attendant account of the good news of the gospel, and

---

[5]"In the Incarnation, the Church proclaims the complete divinity and humanity of Christ not for their own sake, but for the sake of the other. The Incarnation demands that God truly *is* man, that it is truly *God* who is man, and that it is truly *man* that God is." Thomas Weinandy, "The Re-emergence of the Human Jesus," in *The Likeness of Sinful Flesh: An Essay on the Humanity of Christ* (Edinburgh: T&T Clark, 1993), 107.

this too, in broad strokes, is shared across the three Christian traditions. The truth about God—Father, Son, and Holy Spirit—is shared Christian truth. The true God is the God of the gospel.

GOOD NEWS

God is the God of good news (the meaning of the word *gospel*). Any so-called Christianity that is not good news is simply not Christian. The triune God is good. The Father is good, the Son is good, and the Holy Spirit is good. God's work in Israel—and, through Israel, God's work in every nation—is good work. The life-changing news of what the Father has done in the Spirit through the Lord Jesus Christ is good, good, good news.

The good news of the gospel centers on Israel's Messiah, Jesus Christ, and on what he has done in his incarnation, life, death on the cross, and resurrection (1 Cor 15:3-8). As an Israelite, Jesus brings the good news of the God of Israel (2 Tim 2:8) promised in the Scriptures, to all the nations (Rom 1:1-6). The gospel of this Jesus "is God's saving power for everyone who believes, for the Jew first and also for the Greek" (Rom 1:16). In Jesus, sin and death are defeated, and all are invited into God's righteousness. We live out this good news in unity as the people of God (Phil 1:27). The gospel is good news for all creation, for "every creature under heaven" (Col 1:23).

This good news calls us to repentance and to new life in the kingdom, which has come near in Jesus (Mk 1:14-15). The kingdom is good, unlike the kingdoms of this world. The kingdom is a blessing to the whole world, open to all, a kingdom of justice and peace. The good news demands a kingdom-shaped response; we hear "the word of truth" and respond with trust; God marks us "with the seal of the promised Holy Spirit" (Eph 1:13). The good news of the gospel transforms lives (Rom 15:16) in ways no human power could accomplish, in ways that can happen only through the power of God (1 Thess 1:5-6). The good news is to be proclaimed wherever Christ is not known (Rom 15:20), for good should not be hoarded. Good news is meant to be shared.

The good news is not obvious. It runs contrary to expectations, "for the message about the cross is foolishness to those who are perishing" (1 Cor 1:18). The good news "is not of human origin" (Gal 1:11); rather, it comes to us from the good and true God. The good news can be gotten wrong (Gal 1:16); it can be falsified, and false gospels tell lies about who God is and what God's work in the world looks like. The gospel is not some private, interior matter; it invites us into new life, new community, a new world; so says René Padilla:

> The gospel of Jesus Christ is a personal message—it reveals a God who calls each of his own by name. But it is also a cosmic message—it reveals a God whose purpose includes the whole world. It is not addressed to the individual per se but to the individual as a member of the old humanity in Adam, marked by sin and death, whom God calls to be integrated into the new humanity in Christ, marked by righteousness and eternal life. The lack of appreciation of the broader dimensions of the gospel leads inevitably to a misunderstanding of the mission of the church. The result is an evangelism that regards the individual as a self-contained unit—a Robinson Crusoe to whom God's call is addressed as to one on an island— whose salvation takes place exclusively in terms of a

relationship with God. It is not seen that the individual does not exist in isolation, and consequently that it is not possible to speak of salvation with no reference to the world of which he or she is a part.[6]

The real gospel is counterintuitive, countercultural, and so counter to the evil of sin and death. It points us always away from "the desire of the flesh, the desire of the eyes, the pride in riches" (1 Jn 2:16) and toward the way of Jesus:

> who, though he existed in the form of God,
>> did not regard equality with God
>> as something to be grasped,
> but emptied himself,
>> taking the form of a slave,
>> assuming human likeness.
> And being found in appearance as a human,
>> he humbled himself
>> and became obedient to the point of death—
>> even death on a cross. (Phil 2:6-8)

This gospel is not that of pride and power. It is that of the Lord who emptied himself for our sakes. As such, this gospel is so priceless and so powerful that it is worth losing one's life for, and it is so challenging to the world that it may result in that loss of life. But resurrection—and not loss—is the gospel's final good word (Mk 8:35).

Good: I keep saying it. Good, good, good. But goodness is not the whole truth about what we live through day to day. This world groans under the weight of sin. We are broken. We are

---

[6]C. René Padilla, *Mission Between the Times: Essays on the Kingdom* (London: Langham Global Library, 2010), 26.

unable to fix ourselves or this world. We are weeping. We are sinners (Rom 3:23), and we are sinned against. Injustice, oppression, and violence reign, and the vulnerable are pressed down under the feet of those with worldly power. We flee from God. We do harm. We turn, in pride, to our own power, and we worship false idols of staggering variety. We mourn, and we grieve. The world is full of abuse and pain and suffering. How can I even say the word *good*?

I say it in faith that the God of good news brings good news to just this world of pain. The gospel is good news for sinners who cannot save themselves. The gospel is good news for mortals who grieve our dead. The gospel is good news for the oppressed and the suffering. The gospel is our good God's promise to make all things new. In Jesus, sin and death are being undone.

On the cross, he has held our sin (1 Pet 2:24), and in the resurrection we are united with Jesus in the new life of the kingdom (Rom 6:5-6). We are forgiven (1 Jn 1:9) and made new (2 Cor 5:17). Utterly *unlike* any religion that asks people to do good in order to appease some deity, the Christian gospel acknowledges the deep brokenness of the world and of human beings. That gospel tells the truth about our inability to make things right on our own terms. This means the Christian gospel is that of grace. It is the gospel of the God who chooses to heal and restore us as a gift. In the gospel power of the Spirit (Acts 1:8), God's people are empowered to "do justice and to love kindness and to walk humbly with . . . God" (Mic 6:8).

I am a Christian because I cannot live with evil and suffering. I need hope. I need to know that God hates evil. God is the one who is undoing it, and God is the one who will finally "wipe every tear from their eyes. Death will be no more; mourning and crying and pain will be no more" (Rev 21:4), and we will see the good God of the gospel reigning in truth, love, and power, over this good world, created by God's good will.

So, I am a Christian because of God's work in my story, because of the beauty of the universal Christian faith, and because I trust the God of the gospel. Of course, the reasons I am a Christian entail more than reason alone. They include heart and spirit, body and soul, the whole of human being. Christian faith embraces logic, but it is not only a logical exercise. If God is God, if Christian faith is true, it will have to be embraced by faith and not by sight.

TWO

WHY I AM PARTICULARLY PROTESTANT

IF I AM A CONVINCED CHRISTIAN, why go on to claim and affirm a particular kind of Christianity? If the beauty of the gospel of Jesus Christ is the shared treasure of all Christian traditions, why adhere to one tradition? If the grace by which I believe I am being saved is the grace of Christ and not the grace of some false god interested only in Protestant Christians, why hold to the Protestant tradition? Why do I claim Protestantism in particular?

This question has been pressing in my own experience, because a key aspect of my academic theological formation and a good part of my adulthood has involved watching people I care about—my doctoral adviser, close friends, students, and my parents—convert (or *move*; I'm not sure *conversion* is the best word here, but it is the one we generally use) from Protestant to Roman Catholic Christianity. This kind of Protestant-to-Roman Catholic spiritual journey is not unusual, especially in certain circles, for committed Christians in our time.

There's plenty of Protestant speculation about the appeal of Roman Catholicism (and, less frequently in the US, Orthodoxy) for certain Protestants. The twentieth century saw great interest in Christian unity in many theological circles. Many Protestants have grown disillusioned with the fragmentation some see as inherent to Protestantism. They have tired of endless splits and splits again, and they are drawn to a church that claims a clear and visible institutional unity. Some Protestants have come to see the traditions in which they have moved as impoverished versions of Christianity, having been so stripped of history and tradition, sacramentalism and liturgy, that people sometimes feel the way to find the fullness of the faith is to turn to a church that claims ancientness in a more obvious way than can any Protestant denomination (or nondenomination) founded only in recent centuries or even decades.

Christians moving away from Protestantism are also often motivated by frustration with the difficulties involved in interpreting Scripture and claiming Scripture as the chief authority for faith. Faced with the seeming impossibility of solving many debates about how to interpret Scripture, some are drawn away from Protestantism to the clear and seemingly straightforward accounts of how authority operates in Roman Catholicism. Such conversions may also be motivated by a sense that Protestantism has given up on the mystical riches of church history in favor of something more bare and rationalized. (As with all moves, those who move away from Protestantism are also sometimes surprised by how much less clear, straightforward, and beautiful things look in the actual church on the ground in their new ecclesial homes.)

Given what I have said about the shared riches of the faith, I don't view exits from Protestantism in favor of Roman Catholic or Eastern Orthodox Christianity as something to mourn. Whenever followers of Jesus discern paths that will help them walk in true discipleship and praise, I rejoice for those fellow Christians. But I also do not accept the claim that Roman Catholicism and Eastern Orthodoxy offer better accounts of church unity, truth, and authority than Protestantism can. In a climate where conversions away from Protestantism claim the riches of history and, sometimes, a sure account of authority, Protestantism can even begin to seem like the least interesting way to be a Christian, a kind of immature and intellectually weak faith. I am not kidding when I say that in some circles, being Protestant just does not seem very sexy.

But I have long known that such a conversion will not be my path. I have remained gratefully Protestant, while growing in conviction about core confessions of the classic Protestant tradition. In fact, I have wanted to write this book for a long time: a book that rejoices in shared Christian faith across Christian traditions but is also very clear and unapologetic about Protestant conviction. This book stands up for Protestantism in a time where it is easily dismissed. With writer John Green, I confess that "it's been my experience that almost everything easy to mock turns out to be interesting if you pay closer attention."[1] I do not accept the accounts of Protestantism (as impoverished, as hopelessly fragmented) described above. On the contrary, I find in Protestant faith the most faithful and livable account of what it means to be a disciple of Jesus Christ. In the rest of this chapter, I explore how I understand Protestant Christianity as catholic, orthodox, and reformed, along with ways I am convinced that Protestantism is the most faithful way to live a catholic, orthodox, and reformed faith.

---

[1]John Green, "The Indianapolis 500," in *The Anthropocene Reviewed: Essays on a Human-Centered Planet* (New York: Dutton, 2021), 170.

PROTESTANT BECAUSE CATHOLIC

I am particularly Protestant because I am a committed catholic. The Protestant tradition is the only coherent way I see to embrace the unity and catholicity of the actual historic church as enjoined by Scripture and affirmed in the Apostles' and Nicene Creeds, the latter of which attests to faith in "one, holy, catholic, and apostolic church."

What Protestant child (at least in the sort of Protestant church that recites creeds) hasn't asked, "Why do we say that? We're not Catholic." And the standard answer, which Protestant parents and Sunday school teachers probably learned from their parents and Sunday school teachers, is that "catholic—with a lowercase *c*—means universal."

And so it does. The church catholic is the universal church, the whole church, the church to which God has gifted all of what the church needs to be the church, the church in every time and place. The Roman Catholic Church tradition claims to be *the* catholic church and narrates history such that every other church is guilty of rupturing the catholicity that rests in Rome. But we need not accept that narration, and I do not find said story persuasive.

When the late medieval Roman Catholic Church accused Martin Luther, father of the Protestant Reformation, of schism, of breaking catholicity, he turned the accusation around, saying that any break in catholicity came from Rome, because Rome had failed to embody church faithfully.[2] Late medieval Roman Catholicism and the earliest emergent Protestantism were

---

[2]Luther says this all over his works; for example, see "On the Babylonian Captivity of the Church," in *Martin Luther's Basic Theological Writings*, 3rd ed., ed. William R. Russell and Timothy F. Lull (Minneapolis: Fortress, 2012), 196-223.

operating with different definitions of catholicity. While most Protestants today rightly eschew the strong condemnatory rhetoric Luther used against Rome (and Rome against Luther), I remain persuaded by his Protestant vision of catholicity.

Roman Catholicism understands catholicity as resting in unity with Rome under the authority of the pope, as the bishop of Rome. I will call this "institutional unity," because it locates unity in shared key institutions. A Protestant vision of catholicity locates the unity of the universal church in the church's faithful reception of the gifts God intends for us as God's people. We could call this "unity in practice." Luther believed the Roman Catholic Church of his time and place to be guilty of violating catholicity by failing to faithfully receive those gifts, especially in failing faithful proclamation of the Word, which Luther saw as having been twisted by church adherence to human traditions over against the Word of God and by a system of works-based righteousness that materially benefited Rome.[3] He also saw the Roman Catholic Church of his time as failing at faithful administration of the sacraments. On Luther's account, that church failed, here by a mistaken theology that understood the church, rather than Jesus, to be the mediator between God and us, again to the material benefit of Rome.

For Luther, true catholicity was and is found where the church receives God's gifts, especially Word and sacrament, in faith. Those gifts are received for the sake of the gospel of Jesus Christ. Luther thus maintained that the Protestant churches simply *were* the catholic church. They could claim that

---

[3]See David C. Steinmetz, *Luther in Context*, 2nd ed. (Grand Rapids, MI: Baker Academic, 2002); and Heiko A. Obermann, *Luther: Man Between God and the Devil*, trans. Eileen Walliser-Schwartzbart (New Haven, CT: Yale University Press, 2006).

catholicity because they were attending to the wholeness of what God has for the church. On this vision, the Protestant church was not something new but was standing in unity with the faithful church throughout the ages. I find this emphasis on the wholeness of the church helpful in continuing to imagine what it might mean for all churches, including Protestant churches, to claim catholicity.

I also want to account for the universality of the church in a way I do not see as historically viable on a Roman Catholic account of catholicity. The catholic church is the church universal, spread across centuries and continents, time and space. The whole church *just is* the catholic church. I believe theology must take historical reality seriously, and so I cannot accept a definition of catholicity that would exclude any instance of faithful church from belonging fully to the church catholic. Historically speaking, there just was a church *before* the Roman Catholic Church existed. There was a church before bishops existed, in the Roman Catholic sense, a church before the priority of the bishop of Rome (the pope), a church before Roman Catholic tradition was codified in the many documents now taken as definitive for Roman Catholic teaching.

Many would narrate history otherwise, as though there were a "once upon a time" in which unity was simple and clear, without cracks. This is the standard Roman Catholic narrative, often repeated by Protestants. For example, Peter Leithart claims, "Once there was just 'the church.'"[4] While I admire Leithart's sincere desire to press us all toward church unity, this account is not historically persuasive. In reality, there was and

---

[4]Peter Leithart, *The End of Protestantism: Pursuing Unity in a Fragmented Church* (Grand Rapids, MI: Brazos, 2016), chap. 1, Kindle.

is no pristine church, existing before and behind dissent, difference, and diversity.

This does not require us to give up on unity. Even when the New Testament was written, there was dissent in the church, but that dissent is not to be understood as ultimate division, because it is enfolded in the one work of God. Though "one says, 'I belong to Paul,' and another, 'I belong to Apollos'" (1 Cor 3:4), Paul dismisses the idea that these followings might undo the oneness of the church; "I planted, Apollos watered, but God gave the growth" (1 Cor 3:6). Here, catholic unity rests in the work of God, full stop. That unity is not something humans can destroy. The New Testament account of church is always one of diversity in unity, unity in diversity, and so our accounts of continued catholic unity can and must allow for difference: "For just as the body is one and has many members, and all the members of the body, though many, are one body, so it is with Christ. For in the one Spirit we were all baptized into one body—Jews or Greeks, slaves or free—and we were all made to drink of one Spirit. Indeed, the body does not consist of one member but of many" (1 Cor 12:12-14).

The church grew and thrived in areas of the world that would never come under Roman Catholic authority. I cannot accept an account of catholicity that would count the Ethiopian church or the developing Eastern Orthodox church as somehow less catholic than the Western Roman Catholic one. Later in church history—and one need not go as late as the Protestant Reformation to get there—there are clear instances of church that are not Roman Catholic, and these too I simply must count as belonging to the catholic church. Where God gives gifts to the church—especially Word and sacrament—and where the

Spirit of God works, there I must recognize the one catholic church. "There is one body and one Spirit, just as you were called to the one hope of your calling, one Lord, one faith, one baptism, one God and Father of all, who is above all and through all and in all" (Eph 4:4-6).

All this insistence on broad catholicity does not keep me from being a grump about it. I have my own preferences about how the church should go about being the church, and I even believe there are good biblical and theological reasons to support those preferences, but I simply will not allow myself to define any part of the catholic church (the one wholly equipped by the one God) out of being catholic (part and parcel of the church whole and universal). There are churches that make my skin crawl, churches I find embarrassing, churches I would shudder to enter, and yet, I will maintain by faith that they are the church catholic. I learned this from the great catholic thinker Augustine of Hippo, though I admit I want to push it rather further than he was willing to do.

I'll say more about this in the next chapter, but Augustine's experience as a pastor taught him one important thing about the church: it exists by the grace of God. Augustine's instincts were against this. He was incensed by a breakoff church, the Donatists. He hated those Donatists. He felt their breaking the institutional unity of the church (by the Donatists leaving the imperial church and starting a new church in the desert) as a grievous thing. And it is. Division in the body is always grievous, though which party gets to count the other as the schismatic body is always tendentious.[5]

---

[5]I am happy, for instance, to assert that neither Augustine's imperial catholic church nor the Donatist desert church was the innocent party here.

But Augustine was a theologian of grace, and he ultimately had to admit that what is important about the church must be about God's grace and not about what *we* do in our churches, even about whether we break away for the wrong reasons. If he had denied that God might grace the Donatists as God graces the church, Augustine would have found himself trying to make a perfect church of his own, the same error he was so angry at the Donatists for committing. Augustine's great insight is that the church exists by grace and not by works. If the church matters, it matters because God is at work in it, not because of whatever we humans are getting right or, inevitably, wrong.

I am with Augustine. The church is the church of Jesus Christ only if that church exists by grace and not by works. The church's richness and unity is God's and not ours. The church is empowered and constituted by the Spirit and not by human leaders, teachings, or institutions. This truth demands an account of catholicity that insistently opts for including, not excluding, churches from participating in catholicity.

Catholicity embraces Roman Catholic, Eastern Orthodox, Protestant, and other traditions, but Protestantism understands the church in a way that allows for that embrace. And, yes, catholicity embraces those churches that make me shudder. Protestantism is honest about this. Even as it suffers breaks and dissent, it is inherent to Protestantism to recognize that churches that are not *my* church still *are* church. This does not require rejection of visible church unity, but it will not allow the terms of that unity to be defined by institutional union with Rome. Because the church is catholic, I am a Protestant.

Yet, catholicity cannot mean that the church lacks shape and identity. Catholicity is not an anything goes for the church. This is where Luther was aiming when he claimed that the church was constituted by faithful proclamation of the Word and faithful administration of the sacraments. When the Nicene Creed confesses what the church should be, it calls for more than unity and catholicity. It calls also for the church to be holy and apostolic. The church is supposed to be shaped like Jesus in what the body of Christ does and says, teaches and preaches. The church is supposed to be shaped like Jesus in how that body worships and serves, lives together in community, and loves the world in invitation and mission. The church is called to orthodoxy.

PROTESTANT BECAUSE ORTHODOX

I am particularly Protestant because I love orthodoxy. The word *orthodox* does not have as many fans as it once did. It has come to suggest intolerance, heresy trials, and witch burnings. Orthodoxy is about getting things right (the meaning of *ortho-*), and we've become rightly suspicious of such attempts. We're aware that there are many perspectives, that those who believe in their rightness have so often been wrong, and that ideas of the right can be used—as in heresy trials and witch burnings— to legitimate violence. Such abuses of Christian orthodoxy, however, are themselves unorthodox and even heretical, for they do not rightly witness to the truth of the righteous God. As Stanley Hauerwas has it, when "orthodoxy becomes defensive rather than a form of love and proclamation it denies its own reality. . . . [Orthodoxy] does not require coercion to sustain itself. Rather orthodoxy is displayed as an act of love."[6]

---

[6]Stanley Hauerwas, "Foreword," in *Heresies and How to Avoid Them: Why It Matters What Christians Believe*, ed. Ben Quash and Michael Ward (Grand Rapids, MI: Baker Academic, 2007), x.

The goodness and beauty of orthodoxy can be pursued only in humility. This pursuit requires a keen awareness of human limits. We are limited in our orthodoxy because we are finite. We are not God, and we can never fully know God. Nor can we, as humans, get our understanding of God right. We are also limited by our sinfulness, and orthodoxy thus requires vigilance about our own tendencies to self-righteousness, self-aggrandizement, power and control, blindness to others, disordered desire, and pride. Such vigilance can hope to succeed only where careful structures for accountability are in place and the church is bathed in prayer and self-consciously sustained by the power of the Spirit.

Protestantism contains within itself this directive for humility and these limits, as key aspects of Protestant Christianity include vigilance about and suspicion of human sinfulness and the clear requirement that orthodoxy must be based in revealed Scripture and not on human-made traditions of the church. Where Roman Catholicism and Eastern Orthodoxy must place a great deal of confidence in the church as guardian of orthodoxy, Protestantism is inclined to be suspicious of false churchly orthodoxies, which compete against the orthodoxy revealed in the Word of God. The Protestant slogan "reformed and always reforming" acknowledges our human inability to get things right and commits Protestants to an ongoing process of seeking greater faithfulness to the Word.

Orthodoxy comes from God and not from us. It is a gift of God's choice to reveal God's character and nature to human beings, and so it relies on Scripture as the revealed Word of God. Orthodoxy flows from living in the story of Scripture, and it is best fostered in communities committed to the Protestant principle "Scripture alone." This principle does not mean that Protestants ignore other sources of knowledge of God—including church, tradition, reason, and experience—but it does mean those other sources are secondary to Scripture because they are different in kind from Scripture. Scripture is unique, and in it God reveals righteousness and truth.

Orthodoxy can only make sense if we think of its "rightness" not as a human triumph or a fortress to be defended but as rightness in relationship to the living God. Orthodoxy is not primarily about getting our thinking right. Orthodoxy is built on and lives through right relationship with God. Genuine Christian orthodoxy is about righteousness, which belongs primarily to God and which describes our relationship to God only because we have been brought into right relationship with the Father through the Son in the Spirit. God's righteousness is beauty, truth, goodness, and justice. Orthodoxy is orthodoxy only when it participates in this righteousness of God.

Orthodoxy is not just about right(eous)ness. It is also about praise (the *-dox-* in the word is the same root that begins the word *doxology*, which is to give praise to God):

Praise God from whom all blessings flow.
Praise God all creatures here below.
Praise God above ye heavenly host.
Praise Father, Son, and Holy Ghost.

Here too, orthodoxy is relational. It is about the eternal righteousness and love of the Father together with the Son and the Holy Spirit, and it is about the relationship of righteousness and love Christians are meant to bear to God, to other humans, and to all of creation. We get our praise right when we worship the true and living God. While only a small part of Christian orthodoxy involves articulating theology as statements of truth, that part is centered on the trinitarian and christological claims of the Councils of Nicaea and Chalcedon, because those claims are about rightly identifying the God revealed in the Scriptures of the Old and New Testaments. Orthodoxy helps us to recognize the difference between that true God and endless false idols.

Again, orthodoxy is not only or even primarily about articulating true statements about God. It is about living in right relationship with God, and that includes living in right relationship with other human beings and all of creation. Orthodoxy is a life. It must be embodied. And orthodoxy gives the church its identity. It marks Christianity out as Christian in distinction to other faiths.

Orthodoxy names the divinely intended shape and character of the church of Jesus Christ, asking that church to conform to Jesus and not to the world. The church as holy and apostolic thus treasures orthodoxy. If we are no longer worshiping the true God, we are no longer Christian. The church seeks holiness as we seek to be remade in the image of Christ our Lord. It seeks apostolicity in faithfulness to apostolic teaching, a concept that points to the true and ancient faith, as the apostles who knew Jesus face to face received that faith and passed it on to us. While other traditions locate the apostolic nature of the church in church leaders (e.g., apostolic succession, the pope), the Protestant church seeks apostolicity in faithfulness to Scripture.

PROTESTANT BECAUSE REFORMED

I am particularly Protestant because I pray that I am being reformed. In theology, the word *reformed* refers to the broad affirmations of the Protestant Reformation as well as to a certain theological tradition, a subset of Protestantism. When the word is capitalized, *Reformed* usually denotes a theological system that derives in some way from the theology of John Calvin. While I have a great deal of respect for Calvin and the great magisterial Reformers, I am not a "Reformed" Protestant in that tradition. I am, however, convinced that the key affirmations of the Protestant Reformation and broad "reformed" Protestant theological distinctives are true and are a valuable aid in guiding catholic orthodox Christianity.

To be reformed is to be animated by the Protestant "solas."[7] The Latin *sola* means "alone," and—in a delightful rhetorical move—Protestants affirm a series of them: *sola gratia* (grace alone), *sola fide* (faith alone), *sola Christus* (Christ alone), *sola scriptura* (Scripture alone), *sola Deo Gloria* (to the glory of God alone). Together, these solas testify to the heart of Protestantism, calling the church away from human sin and error and back to God alone. The key epistemological and methodological move in answering this call is to rely on Scripture as *the* normative authority for catholic and orthodox faith and practice.

In calling the church to do this, the Protestant Reformers identified in Scripture an important point of contention with late medieval Roman Catholic faith and practice. Our salvation, the Reformers insisted, does not depend on the church, priests, and sacraments, nor does it depend on human action or meritorious work. Salvation is sheer gift; it comes to us by grace alone, through faith alone, because of Christ alone.

---

[7]See Kevin J. Vanhoozer, *Biblical Authority After Babel: Retrieving the Solas in the Spirit of Mere Protestant Christianity* (Grand Rapids, MI: Brazos, 2018).

The Reformers were not creating something new here. This teaching stood in continuity with the orthodox teaching of the church catholic all along; it had always been key to the shared Christian gospel. In broad terms, the Protestant Reformers were reaffirming the doctrine of salvation taught by Augustine in the fourth century, which had been authoritative for the Western church ever since, and Augustine himself got that teaching from Paul: "For by grace you have been saved through faith, and this is not your own doing; it is the gift of God—not the result of works, so that no one may boast" (Eph 2:8-9).[8]

But—in at least some circles in late medieval Roman Catholicism—that teaching was being distorted in ways that offered a false gospel to the people of God. Salvation was a ladder to be climbed; a purgatory full of agonies loomed large in the Christian imagination for those who failed to reach its top. The church exploited this fear to sell indulgences, which promised to buy time out from that torture chamber. The Inquisition threatened more torture. The Eucharist was meted out according to church hierarchies, and laypeople did not receive the cup. Corruption, cronyism, and nepotism were despoiling the sacraments of the church, and people lived in fear lest they die without the church's last rites. The penitential system encouraged a mechanistic understanding of salvation. Late medieval Roman Catholicism was diverse in belief and practice, and certainly it was never without grace, but Luther struck a chord with many when he denounced the way practices named

---

[8]There isn't space for this here, but I believe this is fully compatible with the best insights of the "new perspective" on Paul, provided one does not insist on false dichotomies or suppose that entire doctrines, such as soteriology or ecclesiology, must be based on first-century concepts alone.

in this paragraph left him and others in fear lest they be cut off from the grace of the church.

Protestant theology cut through this late medieval clericalism and insisted instead that salvation is a gift from God and that no prizes could be earned by performing acts of contrition, buying indulgences, or turning to priests to dispense aid though the offices of the church. Instead, salvation is sheer gift. The rightness of our relationship with God is not attained through anything we might do; it is Christ's righteousness, which is counted as ours because we are united to him in faith. All is grace. Believers were assured that, because of Jesus, we were free to "approach the throne of grace with boldness, so that we may receive mercy and find grace to help in time of need" (Heb 4:16). In terms of soteriology (teaching about salvation), I am unabashedly Protestant. The truth of the good God of Scripture is the gospel of grace. I am convinced that Protestant Christianity offers the most faithful and livable way for the church to follow its call to catholicity, orthodoxy, and reformed faith.

THREE

HOW PROTESTANTISM
HELPS ME BE CHRISTIAN

I TRUST IN all the things I've been talking about so far. There simply is nothing more real or beautiful than the triune God of the gospel. There is no more satisfying account of human life and purpose than that lived in the body of God's catholic, orthodox, and reformed church.

And yet.

Being a Christian is really, really, very, very, super hard. There's doubt, and there's difficulty. There are days when the truth I'm living for is so mocked by lies and evil that I'm tempted to give up hope. Many people, including some in my own profession, consider the idea that we can know who God is and what God wants to be laughable. For some, uncertainty and division are all we can know. Not only is the world full of great evil, but Christians perpetrate evil against others and against one another.

And then there's the reality of the church. Like other truths confessed by Christians, the claim to believe in "one, holy, catholic, and apostolic church" is a claim made by faith and not by sight. Frankly, I find it more challenging to place faith in the church than I do to put faith in the resurrection. The resurrection is sheer beauty, but the body of Christ is so very broken. Though intended for unity, it is rife with division. Though called to holiness, it is mired in ugliness, corruption, and sin. The church inflicts suffering and abuse. Though God offers to gift us with wholeness and truth, we reject those gifts and propagate truncated or twisted distortions of the gospel, narcissistic deformations of leadership, and colonialist parodies of mission. We persist in worshiping idols that bear no resemblance to the holy triune God. We bow down before wealth, sell out orthodoxy for power, and harm the most vulnerable. The reality of the church is not an easy locus for faith.

How can the very people of God breed such evil? In the words of the prophet Isaiah:

> For your hands are defiled with blood
>   and your fingers with iniquity;
> your lips have spoken lies;
>   your tongue mutters wickedness.
> No one brings suit justly;
>   no one goes to law honestly;
> they rely on empty pleas; they speak lies,
>   conceiving mischief and bearing iniquity.
> They hatch adders' eggs
>   and weave the spider's web;
> whoever eats their eggs dies,
>   and the crushed egg hatches out a viper.
> Their webs cannot serve as clothing;
>   they cannot cover themselves with what they make.
> Their works are works of iniquity,
>   and deeds of violence are in their hands.

Their feet run to evil,
 and they rush to shed innocent blood;
their thoughts are thoughts of iniquity;
 desolation and destruction are in their highways.
The way of peace they do not know,
 and there is no justice in their ways.
Their roads they have made crooked;
 no one who walks in them knows peace. (Is 59:3-8)

When the church serves meals of adder eggs and clothes its people in spiderwebs, loving this church is pain. I'm a fan of the AMC show *The Walking Dead*, and I think here of the character Father Gabriel, whose life is shaped by a failure that will always haunt him, having barricaded himself inside his church building while his parishioners begged to come in, trying to escape the zombie apocalypse outside. Gabriel must live with the fact that he saved himself as his people were torn to pieces. From that point on, Gabriel's faith and vocation can only be, for him and for his community, under siege. At times he manages to continue to act as priest, but he's so, so broken. So many people stand outside our church's doors, desperate, while that church refuses their need. We are in a moment of reckoning over church complicity in and perpetration of horrific abuse; the need for this reckoning is one of the biggest crises for contemporary Christian faith.[1] How can I remain a Christian in this church?

I am a Christian because of the triune God, but it sure helps to be Protestant. In Protestant theology, I find hope for true knowledge of God together with an ecclesiology (theology of

---

[1] See Diane Langberg, *Redeeming Power: Understanding Authority and Abuse in the Church* (Grand Rapids, MI: Brazos, 2020).

the church) that allows me to live and work in the midst of churchly sin and brokenness. I'm a Protestant because the church is broken, and it should be inherent to Protestantism that we should not evade full acknowledgment of that brokenness. In the rest of this chapter, I explore three ways Protestant thought helps me be a Christian in a devastated church. First, Protestantism claims the promise of God that we may know God, despite the brokenness of the church. Second, Protestantism encourages an intimacy with and trust in Scripture as the revelation of God and insists that the church of Protestant faith lives by the God of the Word, not by the church's institutions. Finally, Protestantism takes seriously the anti-Donatist theology of the church advanced by Augustine of Hippo, a theology that reminds us that church is church because of God and not because of us. These three things let me live in the mess and difficulty of a church that is not (yet) what God intends it to be.

KNOWING GOD IN A SINFUL WORLD

Increasingly, the very idea that we could access truth about God is portrayed as insular, hubristic, or just plain silly. In this situation, I stand in need of a Protestant doctrine of Scripture, which affirms that our good God wants to be known and chooses to reveal God's character and purposes through the Word. In Protestant teaching about Scripture—and more importantly, in Scripture itself—I meet a God I can trust, assurance of that God's self-identification with the words of Scripture and so of that God's good and trustworthy character, and a way to grow in intimacy with God through the difficulties of life and church and faith. I know a God whose goodness, truth, and beauty assure me that the brokenness of the church is anything but godly. I know a God whose love is so good that it works in that broken church.

Suspicions about our ability to know God are not baseless. After all, God is God, and we are not. Bridging the knowledge gap between the transcendent divine and human finitude is a mighty feat, and the difference between God and us means our ways of knowing God must be different from our ways of knowing created things.[2] We can know a cup of coffee by taste, another person by sight, a symphony by sound, but God must be known by faith, because God isn't a thing among other things. God is God alone, the Lord of the universe, the only eternal one.

We also have reason to question the ability to know God because humans can be very bad at knowing. We're limited, and we're sinful. We're bound in time and space. We revise our science when we learn old theories are wrong, looking back with embarrassment at what we were once certain we knew. We're unreliable narrators, blind to parts of ourselves, and we often act without awareness of our biases and hurts. The realities of human finitude and human sin mean that any knowledge of God is a miracle, and our reception of God's good gift of divine knowledge is always imperfect.

Good Christian theology requires humility in our pretensions to knowledge, but that does not mean we can't know God. If we visit a sad, shoddy zoo (think Netflix's spectacle *Tiger King*) and we peer at a tiger through a filthy glass cage, our knowledge of the tiger will be obscured by the filth. But that doesn't mean the tiger isn't there, pacing in her cage, nor does

---

[2]See Herbert McCabe, *Faith Within Reason* (London: Continuum, 2007).

it mean she isn't knowable in her bright burning and "fearful symmetry."[3] Sin and finitude make the glass murky, but to recognize that we see through a glass darkly is not the same thing as denying the existence of the tiger on the other side of the glass. To know that we now know "only in part" does not mean we won't one day "know fully," precisely because we are in relationship with the one by whom we are "fully known" (1 Cor 13:12). We receive the miracle of the Word in the canon of Scripture, and the fact that we are unreliable interpreters of that Word does not undo God's gift of revelation or close off ways we may faithfully proceed toward more faithful interpretations of Scripture. And it does not account for the ways God works to clear murky glass and heal our powers of knowing. Plus, utterly unlike a tiger, God cannot be caged.

INTIMACY WITH SCRIPTURE, INTIMACY WITH GOD

We don't claim to know God first through intellect or experience. We know God because God acts to make Godself known. Scripture is not the only way God does this. Jesus *is* the decisive revelation of God in history. Scripture is not God, nor does it have the same status Jesus does, but between the first and second comings of Christ, knowing Scripture in the power of the Spirit is our primary mode of revelation about him, and it is to him, together with the Father and the Spirit, that Scripture testifies. God also speaks through nature, through reason, and in the community wisdom of the body of Christ, but Protestant theology recognizes Scripture as different in kind from these other sources of revelation. This is why Protestants affirm

---

[3]William Blake, "The Tyger," in *Songs of Experience*, facsimile reproduction of the 1794 illuminated manuscript (London: William Blake Trust and the Tate Gallery, 2009).

Scripture as the "norming norm," different from and prior to any other authority for Christian faith and life. This is sometimes known as the Protestant principle; *sola scriptura*, Scripture alone, recognizes that knowledge of God must come from Scripture and not from the church, and trusts that Scripture is the revelation needed by a corrupt and broken church.

In Scripture, we meet the triune God. Many other books speak of God, but Scripture is different from other writings, because only Scripture is authored by God. God the Spirit has worked in and with the human authors of Scripture to bring us these words, and so these words are both divine and human in origin. God self-identifies with the very words of Scripture. The authority of Scripture is not a magical property of the text. That authority rests in Scripture's divine author, the God we trust because God is the good Father of our Lord Jesus Christ who empowers us by the Spirit. The authority of Scripture isn't provable; instead, it is known as it operates faithfully in the lives of Christians and the life of the church, guiding us in relationship with the living God and transforming us in the image of Jesus. We rightly call Scripture "the word of God," and that Word is purposeful and powerful; it is for the people of God. Like all knowledge of God, the authoritative nature of Scripture is received in faith, in recognition of what Scripture claims about itself and how Scripture works. "Indeed," says the author of Hebrews, "the word of God is living and active and sharper than any two-edged sword, piercing until it divides soul from spirit, joints from marrow; it is able to judge the thoughts and intentions of the heart" (Heb 4:12).

Because of the gift of divine revelation through Scripture, we have confidence that we know God. This is not a thin knowledge.

Rather, God has revealed truth about God's own character, nature, and work. Scripture doesn't tell us vaguely that some kind of a god might exist. It doesn't permit us to understand God as an anthropomorphic idol (a god made in the image of human beings) or a vague, distant, impersonal power. It renders the character of the triune God—Father, Son, and Spirit—and it tells the story of that God's work among and for human beings in abundant particulars. All human knowing, even knowing by faith, requires a body, and Scripture follows the lead of the incarnation of Jesus in making knowledge of God accessible to our senses as we read and hear and pray that we might embody the Word.

Human beings are bodied creatures, and so we are bodied knowers of God. How wonderful, then, that God should come among us in the flesh and gift to us a word that allows us to know God by bringing us into the story of God's work in the embodied lives of people and nations. Scripture invites us to stand with Eve as she sees the greenness of the garden, with Aaron as he smells the smoke rising from the sacrifices burning on the altars of Israel, with the woman who has been bleeding for more than a decade when she feels the textured fabric of Jesus' robe, with the women and men present at Pentecost as they hear the story of Jesus bubbling out in many languages, with the disciples on the road to Emmaus as they taste the bread of God. We see, smell, touch, hear, taste. And we know God.

Scripture teaches us intimately and deeply of God. Were I called to rely on myself or on the church for knowledge of God, I would despair. But instead, I meet the living God through the living Word. The God I meet there reveals evil, sin, and lies as the evil, sin, and lies they are. Scripture strips those things of pretension to being the truth about God, the world, or God's intentions for the church. They are shown for what they are, in light of the beauty, goodness, and truth of the triune God.

The existence and authority of Scripture is, for me, a kind of theodicy (a way of understanding why evil and suffering plague us so). While it doesn't rationalize evil and suffering according to human logical standards, it demonstrates evil and suffering to be contrary to the creative and redemptive will of the good God, who is making all things new. As a Protestant Christian, I'm unconvinced by a theology that would rely on knowing God primarily through the church and would trust the church as *the* reliable interpreter of Scripture. I find such a theology untenable precisely as a theodicy. For the church, beloved of Jesus, is rotten with sin and riddled with evil. If one is not blind to evil in the church, that church as the rightful authority for knowledge of God can only be an imposter, for the beauty, truth, and goodness we meet in the God of Scripture is not reliably present there. I love the church, and there is no Christian faith outside it. Insisting that the church can't be our first authority does not entail denying the ways church helps us to know God, but to *base* that knowledge there is for me a route to despair, a house on sinking sand. The authority of Scripture opens us to the truth of the triune God and so to joy, goodness, and intimacy with the divine.

PROTESTANT ECCLESIOLOGY

I know the phrase "Protestant ecclesiology" is mocked as an oxymoron. Protestants are widely accused of lacking clear teaching about the church. Such accusations often assume that Roman Catholic and Eastern Orthodox ecclesiology is automatically more robust than anything Protestants can offer, because, after all, Roman Catholicism and Eastern Orthodoxy boast an institutional unity Protestantism cannot claim. But Protestant thought does not grant the assumption that institutional unity (resting in structures, leaders, and teaching offices) is the right way to think about ecclesiology. Further, as I argued above, I don't accept Roman Catholic or Eastern Orthodox claims to greater catholicity because those claims can't account for the facts of God's work in the diverse, visible, historic church as it exists in the world.

In a diverse church in a diverse world, I am comforted and sustained in my faith by Protestant ecclesiology. More, I need Protestant ecclesiology. Without it, I don't know how I could keep going when faced with the sin of the church. While it is true that Protestantism is not always explicit about its doctrine of the church and that Protestant churches face many difficulties, a strong, extremely concrete—visible and embodied—and theologically sound ecclesiology is embedded in Protestant thought. We can learn of that ecclesiology in starting with Scripture and looking to its expression in two important moments in history: with Augustine of Hippo in the late fourth century and the Protestant Reformers of the sixteenth century.

Biblically speaking, ecclesiology is not the clearest of doctrines. It's not that Scripture fails to equip the church, but the biblical witness does resist systematization around many ecclesiological questions that now occupy contemporary theologians. Scripture, in its complexity, resists being read as authorizing a single form of church government or church leadership.[4] The biblical texts are too contextual, too diverse, and

---

[4] I know many Protestants disagree, and I'm not denying there are good reasons for advocating specific models of church governance or leadership, but I don't find clear warrant for

too early in the history of the church to be made sense of in this way.

Those biblical texts do help us to wisdom on such questions, but they don't mandate one system, certainly not a system of authoritarian hierarchy, and they don't establish an ecclesiology that depends on institutions. The institutional church (at least in its highly developed Roman Catholic and Eastern Orthodox forms) is possible only in contexts where the church is not persecuted, which is to say, not possible in the New Testament era. This is not to say that institutions are necessarily bad for the church but that the church cannot be identified with any one institution, such as that of the papacy. This is good news, because it means the church can and must be flexible and contextual in order to serve the diverse needs of this big, God-beloved world.

What the biblical witness does make clear about ecclesiology is that the church is close to God's heart; the church matters (Rom 12; 1 Tim 3); in fact, church is nonnegotiable. Christian faith is communal faith. And the biblical witness also makes it clear that the church of God is both unified and diverse (1 Cor 12), that church is God's good way of working in the world in this eschatological age of the Spirit, who empowers that church and gives it gifts (Acts 2; 1 Cor 13), and that church unity is unity with Christ, an idea imagined through two central metaphors: church as body (1 Cor 12; Eph 1:22-23) and church as bride (Eph 5; Rev 19). The church is the family of those who

---

one system from the biblical text. I would even suggest that Protestant attempts to baptize specific, institutional forms of church government are hangovers from medieval Roman Catholic ecclesiology, leftover instincts to justify Protestant ecclesiology on Roman Catholic terms, but that line of argument takes me down a more particular and polemical path than I want to take in this book.

have been adopted of the Father through the Son in the Spirit (Eph 2:19; 1 Jn 3), born of God, and made "joint heirs with Christ" (Rom 8:17). The one church of Jesus Christ takes diverse forms in particular times, places, and communities. Augustine— one of my favorite theologians—was not comfortable with that idea, but he still recognized the theology of grace that requires it.

Augustine is often claimed by the Roman Catholic tradition, while he's not very popular in Eastern Orthodoxy, but he is a church father for us all. Augustine's catholic church is the Latin-speaking church of the late ancient Roman Empire. While Augustine and that church shaped what would later become the medieval Roman Catholic Church through to the Roman Catholic Church of today, that church was not yet the Roman Catholic Church the Protestant Reformers would speak against a thousand years later. Augustine presumes the catholic unity of the church of his empire, but the church of the fourth century was no more undivided than is the church today.

Augustine was well acquainted with church division, especially through the Donatist controversy, and it was the most important factor to shape Augustine's ecclesiology. Augustine's thinking in response to the Donatist church has proved central to Western—both Roman Catholic and Protestant—ecclesiology ever since. The church at the time was still emerging from intermittent periods of persecution under the Roman Empire. While the emperor Constantine's conversion to Christianity in AD 312 changed the relationship between the church and that empire forever, emperors after Constantine were not uniformly friendly to Christian faith.

The Donatist church arose in response to one of those times of persecution. Under the emperor Diocletian, Christian leaders were asked to prove loyalty to the emperor by burning the Christian Scriptures. Many resisted this demand and paid the price as martyrs, but some Christian leaders did comply. Later, when Diocletian was gone and church and empire were again partnered, some of those same people who had burned the Scriptures wanted to be reinstated to their leadership positions in the church. In Augustine's imperial church, they were able to do so. Repentance and restoration were deemed possible.

Imagine how this would have felt if you were a Christian who had stood faithful throughout the time of persecution. Imagine how it would have felt if someone you loved had suffered death at the empire's hands for refusing the emperor's loyalty test. The Donatists refused to accept the restoration of those unfaithful leaders as priests of the church. They wanted a pure church leadership, and they rejected the imperial church to create another church in the desert. Scholars disagree about how sociological factors contributed to the Donatist split, but it's possible the Donatists also represented native North Africans rejecting an imperial church.[5] The history of the Donatist controversy is blood spattered on both the Donatist and imperial sides. There are no clean hands there, certainly not Augustine's. Fortunately, Augustine also gave us an ecclesiology that can handle the ugly facts.

If you're like me, you're not unsympathetic to the Donatists. Standing under a church leader who had betrayed the faith to save his skin would be a hard thing to swallow. Augustine, however, was not sympathetic at all. For him, the Donatists stood guilty of dismembering the very body of Christ. They

---

[5]See Justo L. González, *The Mestizo Augustine: A Theologian Between Two Cultures* (Downers Grove, IL: IVP Academic, 2016).

were mutilating the church and placing themselves outside the one people of God, whose unity Augustine very much understood in the institutional sense I've already disavowed.

His strong feelings here led him to bless the use of imperial force against the Donatists, in attempts to force them to return to the imperial church, and that decision was a tragic one. It was used for centuries to legitimate Christian collaboration with national and military might. Again, I'm repulsed, and I find myself in need of an ecclesiology that can handle the sin and ugliness of church history without denying that sin and ugliness. I need an ecclesiology for an impure church. In the time and place in which I write, the impulse to a Donatist purity seems rampant both in the world at large and in the church. One wrong move, if it is the right wrong move, can condemn a person and their work forever. Churches split in efforts to separate from impurity, even while both sides see themselves as the pure one.

I find it curious that the Donatist controversy and Augustine's role in it are often preached as a morality tale in favor of Roman Catholic institutional unity. Certainly, Augustine wished for that unity (though, again, his catholic church cannot be simply identified with the high-institutional Roman Catholic Church of the late Middle Ages). But the positive theological content to emerge from Augustine here is not his contempt for Donatists and insistence that they rejoin his institution. The theological gold of the Donatist controversy is not Augustine's horror at institutional division. Instead, it is found in his insight into the work of grace, even in a church he deemed theologically disastrous. Augustine the pastor faced a practical question. Could God be at work among the hated Donatists?

Answering this question centered on baptismal practice. If Julia had been baptized in the Donatist church but later wished to join Augustine's church, was her schismatic baptism valid? I imagine how much Augustine wanted to say no! How could he accept anything that came out of those who were rending the unity of the body of Christ? I imagine him sickened by the irony of his predicament. The error of the Donatists rested in trying to create a pure church, trying to count as leaders only those who had not sinned. If Augustine refused to accept Julia's separatist, Donatist baptism, he would be doing the same thing the Donatists had done—insisting the church must get things right in order for it to be the church.

I imagine Augustine gritting his teeth as he comes to his (completely necessary) conclusion. Julia's baptism must count. Whatever is important about baptism is about the work of the Holy Spirit and not the human church leaders where the baptism occurs. Whatever makes the church the church is God's work and not ours. Whatever matters in what the church does matters because of the grace of God and not because of the validity or purity of the human beings involved. Augustine is best known as a champion of God's grace, a reputation sealed later in his life when he insisted against Pelagius that human beings are so broken by sin that we can be saved only by the healing grace of God. But Augustine was also the theologian of grace in his response to the Donatism, which we might see as Pelagianism writ ecclesial.

The church is a church of grace and not of works. That's Augustinian gold, and it's as true today as it was in the ancient world. God must be acknowledged as working in the impure Donatist church. Augustine's ecclesiology of grace became normative for the church in the West, and it remains normative for the Roman Catholic Church today. While the Roman Catholic Church understands itself to be *the* catholic church in a special way, it acknowledges the work of God outside its bounds. (If I were to convert to Roman Catholicism, the church would accept my Protestant baptism as valid.)

But Roman Catholic theology does not take Augustine's ecclesiology of grace as far as it needs to go. While acknowledging God's work outside Roman Catholicism, said Catholicism also teaches that the Roman Catholic Church is without sin. I find Roman Catholic belief in the sinlessness of the church untenable in the face of reality. Roman Catholic ecclesiology stakes a great deal on institutional structures, including on the priority of the pope, the reliability of church tradition, and the church as a mediator of grace. Augustine's theology of grace has taught me these things must be called "works." Such an institutional version of purity cannot account for the diversity of the work of God among the church bodies of the world.

Protestant ecclesiology is the necessary flowering of Augustine's ecclesiology of grace. If God can and does work in corrupt places, who are we to limit the church to our own institutions and borders? If every historical church is riddled with sin, who are we to claim the rightness of our own churches? But if church is grace, then Protestant churches are church. More, they are church with the very important mission of promulgating the good news that church is powered by God and not by us. The church is the church by grace and not by institutional structures.

Here someone will object again that I'm not telling the whole of the story of the Donatist controversy. Yes, it led Augustine to accept Donatist baptism as valid, but haven't I underplayed

Augustine's deep concern for the visible unity of the church of Jesus Christ? Doesn't the moral of the story have to be: Okay, yes, God works outside the visible unity of the church, but that visible unity is key and the Donatists were schismatic!? I do believe that the visible unity of the church is vital to an ecclesiology that can sustain us in this broken world. The church can't be what it's supposed to be and do what it's supposed to do unless it is recognizable in the world. We must be able to see and touch the church if we are to be able to identify the one church of Jesus Christ. We must be able to see and touch the church if the church does indeed matter.

So my heart is with Augustine on the importance of visible unity, even if I don't agree with him about the best ways to imagine and live that unity, and it's true that Augustine located the visible unity of the church in much the same way the Roman Catholic Church does today. This is why the theological payoff of the Donatist story is so often misread as "Don't break off into the desert" when the actual payoff is "Don't discount God's work in the desert." Augustine spends a lot of ink saying the first thing, but it's the second thing that is theologically mandated and necessary to ecclesiology. It's the second thing that was a new contribution to theology that would matter for the church going forward. Augustine found unity in institutional building blocks such as the existence of bishops, their accord on church teaching, and their oversight of the liturgy, but his own insight suggests that such an identification of church unity—at least in rigid form—can lead only to a kind of Donatism, to a purist and so works-based ecclesiology. That is, it will require saying something like, "My church has the gifts of God, and yours does not. My church is the holy one." Thus, we lose Augustine's ecclesiology of grace and the strength it gives us for life in a sinful world. Even in Augustine's day, claims to institutional unity were mooted by actual institutional difference. The East existed. The churches that today we call non-Chalcedonian existed. Churches that Western church history rarely narrates and may know nothing of existed.

But what if visible unity is not the same as institutional unity? What if we can imagine visible, embodied church unity on fundamentally different grounds? Augustine didn't imagine an alternative way of conceiving the visible unity of the church, but about a thousand years later, Protestants did. Protestantism must claim this history while continuing to insist that the visible church matters. If we can't identify the church, if we can't see it and touch it, then the church cannot do what we are supposed to do in the world (Mt 28:19; Acts 1:8). We can't be the body of Christ without a visible body.

Roman Catholic and Eastern Orthodox concepts of visible unity as resting in institutional structures are not the only possibilities, and I find the Protestant concepts key to faith, as they fit with an ecclesiology of grace and avoid the real danger of authorizing structures that are at best contingent and at worst sinful. Protestant concepts better make sense of the way God loves and works in diverse contexts around the world. Two Protestant concepts of visible church unity are especially helpful to me: church unity in action and church unity in historic connection to Christ as the root of the church.

FOUR

||||||||||||||||||||||||

DOING CHURCH

Augustine's anti-Donatist ecclesiology of grace served the Christian West for about a thousand years. It was—and is—sturdy stuff. But the time came when it was no longer adequate, by itself, to help the body of Christ imagine and enact our visible unity in the world. The Reformation required new ways of imagining church unity. The church on earth had *always* encompassed difference, but the events of the Reformation meant that the West could no longer pretend otherwise.

When we could no longer ignore the vital existence of Christian churches that rejected unity with Rome, Protestant thought offered two imaginative alternatives, alternatives that can make sense of church unity under conditions in which many Christians could no longer, in good conscience, remain under the authority of the pope. From Martin Luther and the Reformation tradition emerging on the European continent, we learned to imagine church unity as unity in faithful practice: ecclesiology as "church in action." In the English Reformation, we glimpsed the possibility of imagining historic unity that is at the same time adequate to historic and contextual diversity; we'll play a bit loose with the Anglican Church's understanding of the terms and refer to this as "branch ecclesiology." Neither of these ecclesiologies comes to us with a clean history, but such is exactly what we expect if we are practicing an ecclesiology of grace. These two Protestant concepts offer ways of embracing church diversity and context such that we can celebrate God's work in the world and among the one priesthood of all believers, even as we dwell with and in both regrettable brokenness and healthy diversity.

CHURCH AS ACTION

Martin Luther did not admit the Roman Catholic charge that Protestants had broken the unity of the church, and he creatively rethought ecclesiology to explain why. Luther located the visible unity of the church in faithful Christian practice. He did not accept the Roman Catholic claim that unity must be vested in the pope and the institutional structures of the church. Instead, Luther tendered a vision of church unity found in the active gospel faith of the body. The body of Christ is not a body at rest. It moves. It testifies. It acts. It happens and reaches out, and it nurtures those who already are within it.

For Luther, the most important practices of the church were proclamation of the gospel and administration of the sacraments. He argued that the Roman Catholic Church had broken the unity of the body by failing to preach the gospel of grace and failing to faithfully administer the sacraments as sacraments of grace. "The true treasure of the church," said Luther, "is the most holy gospel of the glory and grace of God. But this treasure is naturally most odious, for it makes the first to be last."[1] Luther

---

[1] Martin Luther, "The Ninety-Five Theses," in *Martin Luther's Basic Theological Writings*, 3rd ed., ed. William R. Russell and Timothy F. Lull (Minneapolis: Fortress, 2012), 8.

insisted that church unity rested in faithful gospel preaching, in baptism, and in nurturing the people at the table of the Lord. Where the church faithfully preaches, baptizes, and feeds, there church unity is found, whether the church is institutionally Roman Catholic, Protestant, Eastern Orthodox, or something else. Here we see Luther's characteristic Protestant emphasis on the priority of the Word over any other claim to authority:

> But when they [Roman Catholics] are asked: What is the Christian church? What does it say and do? They reply that the church looks to the pope, cardinals, and bishops. This is not true! Therefore we must look to Christ and listen to him as he describes the true Christian church in contrast to their phony shrieking. For one should and one must rather believe Christ and the apostles, that one must speak God's Word and do as St. Peter and here the Lord Christ says: He who keeps my Word, there is my dwelling, there is the Builder, my Word must remain in it; otherwise it shall not be my house.[2]

Again, Luther rejects the idea that unity must be found in the institutional structures of the church above in "the pope, cardinals, and bishops," and he exhorts us to look to the Word, referenced above as "Christ and the apostles . . . God's Word." Further, we must "do" that Word, living that Word in faith.

This theological move insists that the authority of Peter is the authority of Scripture and not the authority of popes. It reinterprets an important Roman Catholic claim—Peter matters—in a new Protestant direction. In Matthew 16, Peter identifies Jesus

---

[2]Martin Luther, "Sermon in Castle Pleissenburg, Leipzig," in Russell and Lull, *Martin Luther's Basic Theological Writings*, 44.

as "the Messiah, the Son of the living God" (Mt 16:16), and Jesus responds with the words, "On this rock I will build my church" (Mt 16:18). Roman Catholic biblical interpretation identifies the rock as Peter himself, understood to be the first pope, but Protestant interpretation focuses on Peter's confession of who Jesus is. The church is built not on the man Peter but on the teaching and preaching of the identity of Jesus. Peter absolutely matters, and he does so because he faithfully proclaims the scriptural gospel.

As to the "phony shrieking" Luther attributes to his Roman Catholic opponents, we must note that Luther was not a measured man, and his anti-Catholic rhetoric is the sort of language that the book I offer you here rejects. It may help to understand his rhetoric in context if we remember that Catholic authorities were trying to murder Luther at every turn and that Catholics at the time did not characterize Protestants in warm terms either. We also tend to read Luther's rhetoric quite earnestly, but I do wonder whether some of it isn't hyperbole, the rhetorical excess of a man bowled over by the excess of God's grace. Consider Luther's wild take on reliance on baptism as a work disconnected from trust in Jesus:

> The consecrated water is Satan's goblin bath, which cripples, blinds, and consecrates the people without the Word. But in the church one should teach and preach nothing besides or apart from the Word of God. For the pastor who does the baptizing says: It is not I who baptize you; I am only the instrument of the Father, Son, and Holy Spirit; this is not my work.[3]

---

[3] Martin Luther, "Sermon in Castle Pleissenburg, Leipzig," in Russell and Lull, *Martin Luther's Basic Theological Writings*, 45.

The theological point is simply Augustinian; the work of the sacrament is God's work and not the work of the priest or pastor or institutional church. The rhetorical excess is vintage Luther: "Satan's goblin bath, which cripples." While I take Satan and demonic powers seriously, I am not native to the medieval world, and I can't understand just how this bit of rhetoric might have been understood, but it's certainly strong stuff and communicates the seriousness of Luther's theological vision in a way that more careful language might not. (I am *not* suggesting Roman Catholic baptism is Satanic; I agree with Luther; all baptism is the baptism of God. I also agree with Luther; the performance of baptism outside trust in Christ is barren.)

This Luther-ish vision of church unity in faithful action is in no way gnostic, nor is it invisibilist. It is not water that Luther decries; it is the use of water *unbound to the gospel Word*. Luther thinks water is quite a serious matter (whether he really thinks that the sacrament, wrongly administered, might cause blindness, he certainly takes water seriously enough to be deeply concerned about right sacramental practice). And Luther takes the material stuff of the Lord's table seriously. For him, bread and wine are not symbols. They are the very flesh and blood of Jesus Christ our Lord. Here, Luther repeats the Augustinian point also made in the quote about baptism above. The sacrament is given by God and not by the officers of the church. And he adds a fleshy, visibilist, point (one with which Augustine would also agree): the bread and wine matter. The meal feeds us, empowers us, opens to us the grace of God, freely poured out on body and soul: "Likewise, the blessed sacrament is not administered by men, but rather by God's command; we only lend our hands to it. Do you think this is an insignificant meal, which feeds not only the soul but also the mortal body of a poor, condemned sinner for the forgiveness of sins in order that the body too may live? This is God's power . . . not men's."[4]

Luther's church in action is not a gnostic, purely spiritual, interiorized, invisible, and so powerless church. Luther's church in action is *in* the world. It needs to be fed, body and soul, so that it can feed others, body and soul. And while Protestant sacramental theology runs a gamut from Luther's claim that bread is flesh to Zwingli's insistence that bread is symbol, no authentic Protestant ecclesiology can fail to insist that the church must be the *visible* church at work in the world. Personally, my convictions lean here toward Lutheran materialism, but I also believe symbolists when they insist, so rightly, that symbols matter and that symbols too are material. Luther's stark materialism certainly contradicts any claim that Protestant ecclesiology must be doomed to individualist, invisibilist, insubstantial ineffectuality. For Luther, the church is that church in which God comes "to us and we do not need to clamber up to him, he wants to be with us to the end of the world: Here dwells the Holy Spirit, effecting and creating everything in the Christian church."[5]

A Protestant ecclesiology of church in action shows us the church and enacts the one church of Jesus Christ in speaking and sharing the gospel of salvation by grace, dripping with the water of one font and bellies full from feasting at one table. More contemporary Protestant ecclesiology builds on this Reformation vision of unity in church practice, but it seeks to correct what might be in danger of focusing that practice on

---

[4]Luther, "Sermon in Castle Pleissenburg, Leipzig," 45.
[5]Luther, "Sermon in Castle Pleissenburg, Leipzig," 44.

those inside the church at the expense of focusing on the world outside. Such ecclesiology emphasizes unity in church practice as it must be turned outside the church and toward the world. This is often called "missional ecclesiology," and it calls the church to visible unity in mission:[6]

> God made a promise back at the beginning of the biblical story that he would bring about . . . a new world. He chose and formed a community to embody his work of healing in the midst of human history. It was to be a people who could truly say, "I hope some day you will join us" in manifesting the knowledge of God, and the joy, righteousness, justice, and peace of this new world that would one day cover the earth. In this community, one might see the beginnings of the sort of world that God had originally intended in creation, and which he still intended to bring about through his saving work at the end of history.[7]

I find an ecclesiology of unity in practice—both the core internal practices of the church in nurturing the people of God and the constitutive external practice of the church in sharing the gospel and calling others to "join us"—to be invigorating and persuasive. The unity of the church is the unity of a church in action. So, again, Luther:

> And through the interchange of his blessings and our misfortunes, we become one loaf, one bread, one body, one drink, and have all things in common. O this is a great sacrament, says St. Paul, that Christ and the church are

---

[6]See Michael W. Goheen, *A Light to the Nations: The Missional Church and the Biblical Story* (Grand Rapids, MI: Baker Academic, 2011).
[7]Goheen, *Light to the Nations*, 12.

one flesh and bone. Again through this same love, we are
to be changed and to make the infirmities of all other
Christians our own; we are to take upon ourselves their
form and their necessity, and all the good that is within
our power we are to make theirs, that they may profit from
it. That is real fellowship, and that is the true significance
of this sacrament. In this way we are changed into one another and are made into a community by love. Without
love there can be no such change.[8]

CONTEXT, UNITY, AND DIVERSITY

A Protestant ecclesiology of church as action shows us that rejecting the requirement of institutional unity does not mean rejecting unity. From the English Reformation, I'm also helped by
a second Protestant way of articulating church unity, which uses
the metaphor of one tree with many branches for thinking about
the one, visible church of Jesus Christ. Here the unity of the
church is the unity of one, organic organism: a tree with one root.
Jesus is that root, and the churchly rightly and naturally branches
out into different parts of the world, different areas of need. Here
the Roman Catholic, Eastern Orthodox, and Protestant traditions are all healthy branches of one tree, nourished by their living
unity with Jesus Christ. The strength of branch ecclesiology rests
in its dual emphases on the vital life of the church as nourished
by the gospel of Jesus Christ and on the contextuality of the church.

The version of branch ecclesiology that came from the
English Reformation has often been narrowly associated with

---

[8]Martin Luther, "The Blessed Sacrament of the Holy and True Body of Christ," in *Martin Luther's Basic Theological Writings*, 2nd ed., ed. Timothy F. Lull (Minneapolis: Fortress, 2005), 190.

the Anglican Communion, and especially with certain theological programs within Anglican Christianity. Some images of the one tree, which is the church, are somewhat amusing, as the three great branches I just named are portrayed as Eastern Orthodoxy, Roman Catholicism, and the Church of England itself. Many other Christians might see the Church of England as a rather more modest and peripheral branch than such images suggest, including branches of Christianity that also formed on English soil but explicitly rejected the Church of England. This local color, though, need not define the bounds of our imagination for branch ecclesiology. Again and again, God can and does use broken, mistaken things to nonetheless point us to the divine goodness.

When branch ecclesiology imagines the Church of England as a specific, local branch of the one church of Jesus Christ, it does so for local, contextual, and very broken reasons. We are unlikely to understand the kingly contextual reasoning of the English Reformation as legitimate or good. The 1533 Act of Supremacy named the king of England the "the only supreme head on earth of the Church of England."[9] Fulfilling that act, the following is from a declaration of allegiance of bishops and representatives of English clergy to King Henry VIII:

> From henceforth we will promise or give, or cause to be given, to no foreign emperor, king, prince, or prelate, nor to the bishop of Rome (whom they call Pope) fidelity or obedience in word or writing, simple or by oath; but at all times, in every case and condition, we will follow and observe, and to our power defend the parts of your royal majesty, and of your successors. . . . We profess that the

---

[9]Charles Colby, ed., *Selections from the Sources of English History* (London: Longmans, Green, 1899), 145-47.

papacy of Rome is not ordained by God in holy writ, but that it is of human tradition; we constantly affirm, and openly do declare, and will declare, and will diligently take care that others shall so publish the same. Neither will we privately or publicly treat with any mortal man, or give our consent, that the bishop of Rome may here have, or exercise any longer, any authority or jurisdiction, or that he may hereafter be restored to any.[10]

Indeed, why *would* a foreign pope be granted authority over a land not his own, a people not his own? Well, perhaps because said pope might have held Henry VIII accountable for his selfish scheming around his first wife, Catherine of Aragon, and his desired second wife, Anne Boleyn?[11] Perhaps because the doctrine of the divine right of kings seems to you and to me (I imagine) to be ill-conceived, undemocratic, and a failure to grapple with the sinful exercise of power in this world? But perhaps also, from G. W. Bernard, quoting Latimer's account of Anne Boleyn, because Protestants had developed convictions regarding "'detestable slight and frivolous ceremonies' as the pillar of their 'fantastical' religion."[12] Most of this is ugly stuff, but here I am, referencing it unashamedly as I write about hope for Protestant ecclesiology because, again, God can use broken things.[13] To deny this is to deny God's work in the world and the gospel of the grace of Jesus Christ.

---

[10]Colby, *Selections from the Sources*, 145-47.
[11]Lest we kid ourselves, the papacy's defense of Catherine should probably be viewed as rather more political than theological.
[12]G. W. Bernard, "'I Have Done Many Good Deeds in My Life': Anne Boleyn's Religion," in *Anne Boleyn: Fatal Attractions* (New Haven, CT: Yale University Press, 2010), 94-124, here 93.
[13]The conviction against clericalism and extrabiblical authority is not, in my judgment, ugly, but it is important to note that late medieval Roman Catholicism was more diverse than rhetorical excess in said convictions generally accounted for.

I hope we can also imagine very good theological reasons that a local church body might call for local authority and local governance. The history of the demonic welding together of colonial Christianity, imperialism, and slavery could point us in such a direction, regardless of whether our basic ecclesiological sensibilities are more congregationalist or more connectional. While there is no health in disconnecting the local from the universal, the universal church can thrive only if local bodies have the power to attend to, understand, and respond to local cultures, contexts, and needs. Interpretation of Scripture is always contextual, while it also serves the church universal.

Today we see the global church thriving as churches in Africa, Asia, and Latin America move from missionary control to local leadership. I like to imagine Catherine of Aragon and Anne Boleyn smiling together in heaven, having finally seen God take what a king meant for evil and use it for good. It's no accident that so many of these thriving churches are self-consciously Protestant in countries and contexts that have long had a strong Roman Catholic majority. Protestants and Roman Catholics share the good gospel of Jesus Christ, but Protestant ecclesiology is better equipped to embrace and empower the goods of locality, culture, and context, for Protestant theology embraced the local and vernacular four hundred years before Roman Catholic theology did the same.[14]

---

[14] In his recent book, *What It Means to Be Protestant*, Gavin Ortlund makes a similar point: "Because it does not claim to be the 'one true church' but instead positions itself as a renewal movement within her, Protestantism is prepared to discern the true church wherever Christ is present in word and sacrament. Therefore, for Christians seeking to recognize the church in her fullness as we move into the middle of the twenty-first century and beyond, awaiting the return of Christ, Protestantism offers the most promising pathways by which to cultivate and pursue catholicity." Ortlund, *What It Means to Be Protestant: The Case for an Always-Reforming Church* (Grand Rapids, MI: Zondervan, 2024), chap. 3, Kindle.

All kinds of important practical issues are contextual: church structure, modesty, financial practices, the ordering of households, the forming of marriages, the procurement of the elements for the sacrament. Great harm can be done when context and diversity are ignored. God loves context and diversity. Particular things are dear to the heart of the Jesus who took on particularity for our sake and—as a Jewish man in ancient times—embraced the contextual nature of human life in his very flesh. The church is the church of every tribe and tongue and nation, and such differences are not obliterated in redemption. Instead, the redeemed learn to attend to difference, to be strengthened by it, to respect it and care for it. Branch ecclesiology thus fits with the Protestant conviction that the priesthood of all believers is a core part of the good news of Jesus. It seems right that the many branches of the one church should grow out into the world in ways that fit context. This one goes north, that one south. This one needs special nurture because its context is hostile. That one flowers in the abundant sun. All the branches connected to the root will bear fruit. All are alive only because they draw from the one trunk and rely on one solid root system. Branch ecclesiology helps us to imagine a church that is both universal and local, one that draws its vitality from living connection with one root, the Jesus of the gospel.

Picture a tree you know and love. We have a maple in our front yard, which is an ethereal green for a few days each spring before it bursts into full emerald. The image of one tree with many branches has much to recommend it, theologically: as I've just been arguing, the image suits the requirement that ecclesiology be sensitive to both the local and the universal. As an organic image, we can understand it on a gut level. It's an image that fits with the special importance of such organic metaphors in Scripture. Visible unity imagined as a tree with many branches entails an expectation that healthy branches will flourish, for no branch will remain alive if it is not connected to and nourished by the root:

> Abide in me as I abide in you. Just as the branch cannot bear fruit by itself unless it abides in the vine, neither can you unless you abide in me. I am the vine; you are the branches. Those who abide in me and I in them bear much fruit, because apart from me you can do nothing. Whoever does not abide in me is thrown away like a branch and withers; such branches are gathered, thrown into the fire, and burned. If you abide in me and my words abide in you, ask for whatever you wish, and it will be done for you. My Father is glorified by this, that you bear much fruit and become my disciples. (Jn 15:4-8)

This passage, and others that are similar, has unfortunately been used as a crude "fruits test," as though it were a simple thing to identify which individuals and churches are bearing fruit. In ecclesiology, fruits cannot be a test. Fruits are a festival. Yes, a branch can accept so little nourishment from the trunk that it will wither, but it's also true that the one tree flourishes as one tree, one whole, and good gardeners will work to benefit the whole, never cackling in delight that their own branch flowers while another is bare. The branches are not in competition. If one side of my maple is showing disease, this is bad news for the whole tree, not just for that side's branches. The idea that branches that abide in Jesus bear fruit does help us to think about the difference between the healthy, holy church and the church that withers because of disconnection from Jesus, but that thinking is always for the good of the one church. It's for God to prune. The rest of us are to pollinate, to fertilize, and to fruit.

We can't look away from the fact that tree/branch ecclesiology is gospel ecclesiology. As Luther insisted, good trees bear good fruit. That is, it is the God of the gospel of grace who makes the tree what it is: healthy, good, standing in right relationship with God. Fruit bearing is not itself the gospel. Fruit is the result of gospel transformation. Justification precedes and enables sanctification. Luther elaborates:

> It is always necessary that the substance or person himself be good before there can be any good works, and that good works follow and proceed from the good person, as Christ also says, "A good tree cannot bear evil fruit, nor can a bad tree bear good fruit." It is clear that the fruits do not bear the tree and that the tree does not grow on the fruits, also that, on the contrary, the trees bear the fruits and the fruits grow on the trees. As it is necessary, therefore, that the trees exist before their fruits and that fruits do not make trees either good or bad, but rather as the trees are, so are the fruits they bear; so a man must first be good or wicked before he does a good or wicked work, and his works do not make him good or wicked.[15]

GOSPEL MEETS ECCLESIOLOGY

At bottom, I must refuse any ecclesiology that doesn't count every church as church. I must refuse any ecclesiology that isn't

---

[15]Martin Luther, "The Freedom of a Christian," in Lull, *Martin Luther's Basic Theological Writings*, 613.

ultimately about the church existing for the sake of the world. How do we love that world? We do so by being the people of God, bearing witness as the body to God's love for and redemption of broken people, and this requires that our ecclesiology be honest about the brokenness of the church, even as God works redemption there. Ecclesiology must be gospel ecclesiology.

Protestant theology shares some real consensus about the nature of the gospel. At the same time, we Protestants continue to wrestle with the best way to articulate that gospel, especially considering certain deformations of the gospel that have been all too comfortable in Protestant churches and considering the continuing work of reading Scripture well in light of scholarship, contextual needs and insights, and the patient instruction of the Spirit, as that comes with faithful discipleship. Protestant consensus insists that the gospel is grace and not works, highlighting the nature of life in Christ as a gift freely given, not a trophy to be earned. That gift is so free that it's not even a participation trophy. It's a cup overflowing, the living water and the blood of Jesus abundantly pouring out on us, despite what we bring and don't bring. That gift is so free that it is equally for the infant brought to the font with nothing to offer but a wail and the hardened sinner come to the water covered in scars.

When I speak of deformations of the gospel, I'm thinking here especially of those deformations that would allow justification to be cut off from sanctification, making life in Christ into a legal fiction rather than a living, personal, and embodied truth. I'm thinking also of deformations that have sought to control the gospel by forcing it into tidy structures and systems made by humans and then trying to compel conversion through the mechanistic use of those systems. In terms of the continuing work of reading Scripture well, there are endless things to be said, but seeking the unity between classic Augustinian and Reformation perspectives on Paul and "new perspectives" that would have us attend more closely to Jewish contexts is, in my judgment, chief among these. I am convinced of that unity.

While Protestant and Roman Catholic theologies continue to grapple with real differences in understanding the gospel in general and the particular role the doctrine of justification plays in articulating that gospel, it's also true that, since the sixteenth century, we've seen astonishing ecumenical progress. I can happily embrace the following—an excerpt from 1999's *Joint Declaration on the Doctrine of Justification* from the Lutheran World Federation and the Roman Catholic Church—as a summary statement of the doctrine of justification:

> In faith we together hold the conviction that justification is the work of the Triune God. The Father sent his Son into the world to save sinners. The foundation and presupposition of justification is the incarnation, death, and resurrection of Christ. Justification thus means that Christ himself is our righteousness, in which we share through the Holy Spirit in accord with the will of the Father. Together we confess: By grace alone, in faith in Christ's saving work and not because of any merit on our part, we are accepted by God and receive the Holy Spirit, who renews our hearts while equipping and calling us to good works.[16]

I like to imagine Luther and Desiderius Erasmus, sharing a beer in heaven, surprised to find they are happy to embrace this too.

---

[16]Lutheran World Federation and Roman Catholic Church, *Joint Declaration on the Doctrine of Justification* (Grand Rapids, MI: Eerdmans, 2000), 15-16.

Protestants and Roman Catholics share the gospel.[17] Protestants and Roman Catholics share the good news of Jesus Christ, who invites us to share all things with him.

What I am suggesting, then, is that there are important ways in which it is ecclesiology and not the doctrine of justification or the definition of the gospel that makes me Protestant. Not only is Protestant ecclesiology more adequate to naming the sin of the church than is Roman Catholic ecclesiology, but it is more adequate to the good of the gospel, in which grace overflows into works for the sake of the world God loves. If the gospel is the gospel of grace, we need an ecclesiology of grace. There is no ecclesiology of grace without an ecclesiology that is unflinchingly honest about brokenness.

Here, too, there are continuities between Protestant and Roman Catholic ecclesiology. I'm persuaded by Phillip Cary's assessment of Protestant articulations of the gospel as birthed from the best of Catholic ecclesiology, an Augustinian theology of sacrament, which is clearheaded about the objectivity of grace:

> Luther's concept of the Gospel word could not have developed without the medieval Catholic notion of a sacrament as an outward sign that confers the inner gift it signifies. The Protestant Gospel is to that extent a Catholic sacramental notion. Or we could put it more broadly: the Gospel is an external means of grace, and in that regard it is like an Orthodox icon as well as a Catholic sacrament.[18]

---

[17]We should also include Eastern Orthodox Christians and so many Christians who don't fit into those three basic categories in quite the way stories of theology in the West usually narrate them.

[18]Phillip Cary, *The Meaning of Protestant Theology: Luther, Augustine, and the Gospel That Gives Us Christ* (Grand Rapids, MI: Baker Academic, 2019), 203. Also, "According to Luther and a

On Cary's reading of Luther, "Because the word has a sacramental kind of efficacy, it brings with it into the believing heart
the things it speaks of, including righteousness, all the gifts of
grace, and Christ himself."[19]

My colleague Marshall Hatch is pastor of New Mount
Pilgrim Missionary Baptist Church in Chicago. The church's
building once belonged to the Roman Catholic Church, and
the sanctuary retains its gorgeous, vaulted ceilings and much of
the original Catholic art. Saints of the past, though many were
brown in the flesh, are depicted as White Europeans. Those
faces surround the mostly African American congregation
when they meet to worship. The Roman Catholic Archdiocese
of Chicago removed the sanctuary's large rose windows when
they left the building, and the Baptist congregation has replaced
them with stunning African American iconography. The
"MAAFA Remembrance" window is the largest icon of the
Middle Passage in the world; "it pictures an African represen-
tation of Christ whose torso contains the well-known 'Brookes,'
a schematic of a slave-ship first propagated in the late 18th
century." The "North Star—Great Migration Window" "com-
memorates the journeys of African Americans in the 'Great
Migration' of the early to mid-20th century—escaping the
terrors of the Jim Crow Era of racial oppression in the American
South." The third of the rose windows is the "Sankofa—Peace"
window, "referring to the principle of gleaning the wisdom

---

great deal of Protestant theology after him, the Gospel is a saving word of promise that
gives us everlasting life in Christ. This makes it look very much like a Roman Catholic
sacrament, which is an efficacious means of grace that confers the grace it signifies. The
similarity turns out not to be accidental. A sacramental conception of the Gospel is essential to Luther's mature theology" (145).

[19]Cary, *Meaning of Protestant Theology*, 176.

offered from the past, and utilizing it to imagine a better future." The window depicts the four girls murdered in the 1963 Birmingham church bombing together with "the likenesses of contemporary young martyrs of Chicago violence," who "encircle the window's central figure depicting an African Jesus returning the children to a 'Beloved Community.'"[20]

This sanctuary is a powerful ecclesiology, as are those who worship within in that space and within the stories of the Roman Catholic and Missionary Baptist saints depicted on and alive within its walls. The space is continuity between church past and present. The space is broken: windows removed, a past congregation unable or unwilling to maintain ministry when the ethnic makeup of the neighborhood changed. The space is healed: inhabited by a new congregation, by those come through the evil of slavery and the journey of the Great Migration; new windows, themselves depicting the depths of brokenness and the heights of grace, filling the space where the old ones were taken out, like the bands of gold used to repair a broken pot in the Japanese art of *kintsugi*. That highlighted visibility of brokenness and healing is a testimony to grace. It is a visible ecclesiology. I dare anyone to look me in the eye and tell me that New Mount Pilgrim Missionary Baptist Church lacks continuity with the church historic and universal. I dare anyone to claim that church is schismatic. We need Protestantism and Protestant ecclesiology, including ecclesiology as church in action and branch ecclesiology, to answer the very right feeling that none should accept my dare.

---

[20]These descriptions of the windows come from the church's website, New Mount Pilgrim MB Church, accessed July 31, 2023, www.newmountpilgrim.com/gallery. Images of the three windows can be viewed on the site.

FIVE

THE DIFFICULTIES OF PROTESTANTISM

WHILE I REFUSE ACCOUNTS OF CHURCH that reject the viability of Protestant ecclesiology, it would be dishonest to deny the existence of real difficulties within Protestant faith and life. Many would see these as inherent to Protestantism, and there is some truth in that view. Every tradition has innate strengths and weaknesses, and sometimes the same thing is both a strength and a weakness. Undeniably, these difficulties have become typical of Protestantism as it has developed and been practiced over the last five hundred years, particularly in its European and North American expressions. The dangers of individualism, the fragmentation of competing Protestant traditions, and struggles over the operation of authority are all real challenges for Protestant faith. In this chapter, I first examine these three difficulties and then suggest some resources from within Christian faith in general and Protestant faith in particular that can help us live faithfully considering these difficulties.

INDIVIDUALISM, FRAGMENTATION, AND AUTHORITY

In addressing individualism, fragmentation, and authority as difficulties in Protestant faith, it's hard to know which to put first. The three problems overlap and intersect, flowing together, each shaping the others in ways impossible to tease apart. Starting with individualism is a somewhat random choice, though many of the harshest critics of Protestantism would also start here. The worry is this: in shifting the locus of theological authority from church to Scripture, Protestantism elevates the individual as reader and interpreter of Scripture and so changes the lens through which we view who we are and how we relate to God; an ecclesial lens is replaced with an individual one. Instead of thinking about Christian faith as a churchly matter, we come to think of it as an individual choice.

There's no doubt that individualism has gained ground in the West, steadily and steeply, since the Reformation. There's also no doubt that individualism has left indelible marks on Protestant faith, at least in its Western expressions. This is idiomized in contemporary North American Protestant faith in phrases such as "spiritual but not religious," "I like Jesus but not the church," and "personal relationship with Jesus."[1] Whenever I hear that last phrase, I think of the voice of Johnny Cash, booming, condemning and revelatory, as he sings the song "Personal Jesus," which highlights the way the phrase is often about us wanting Jesus to be a kind of tame and unchallenging Santa Claus, there to give us what we want. Such phrases would have been unthinkable for ancient and medieval faith. They

---

[1] This second sentiment is a Ghandian one, written into a popular book title from Dan Kimball, *They Like Jesus but Not the Church: Insights from Emerging Generations* (Grand Rapids, MI: Zondervan, 2007).

would also have been unthinkable for Luther, but he and his fellow Reformers do open doors to hallways that lead to the place where all these sayings are perfectly legible to most people, whether those people embrace faith or not. Still, to decry aspects of medieval Roman Catholic religiosity does not require condemning all religiosity, and Reformation claims against the late medieval Roman Catholic Church are not claims that church itself is dispensable. Protestant faith should long for right religiosity and gospel church, not the elimination of the religious and the ecclesial.

No Christian faith, Protestant or otherwise, can opt for the individual over the communal and continue to dwell within the story of Scripture. From creation, Scripture speaks, "It is not good that the man should be alone" (Gen 2:18), and the story of God's people continues through the Old Testament and into the New as precisely the story of God's *people* and of God's relationship to Israel and to the church *as that people*. We learn that Israel is elect for the sake of others, and those others are not isolated individuals, for God is "a light to the nations" (Is 42:6). The scriptural story teaches us to remember that to be without Christ is to be outside God's *people*: "Remember that you were at that time without Christ, being aliens from the commonwealth of Israel and strangers to the covenants of promise, having no hope and without God in the world" (Eph 2:12). In the reconciling power of Jesus, we are not lone rangers made right with God; we are "fellow citizens with the saints and also members of the household of God" (Eph 2:19). God works in the church, even and especially when that church is broken, and to reduce Christian faith to a loose collection of many separate individuals is as much a wound to the body of Christ as is any church schism.

Yet, schism is closely related to individualism. If the good of the individual is the primary good or is pitted over against the good of the community, it becomes easy to leave the community. We see fragmentation of the church grow steadily from the sixteenth century until we arrive at the landscape of today, wherein the 2018 edition—the fourteenth—of the *Handbook of Denominations in the United States* lists 122 US denominations, including divisions, not just within Protestantism (listing among them twenty-six varieties of Baptists, eight of Methodists, and fourteen "miscellaneous denominations"), but also within Catholic (ten denominations) and Orthodox (twenty variants) traditions.[2]

Making such a list requires many judgment calls, and there are other lists that would take the number of denominations well into the thousands. Some denominations claim to be non-denominations, and many are of obvious interdenominational heritage or commitment. I am a lifelong Methodist who had never heard of Congregationalist Methodists, but there they are, on the list (founded in 1852, with 151 US churches as of 2015), embracing in the name of their denomination something I've always understood as fundamentally alien to Methodist identity.[3] Roman Catholics might refuse to see other claimants to Catholic identity as Catholic at all, but there those churches are, existing and claiming that identity. The three main traditions addressed in this book series (Protestant, Roman Catholic, and Eastern Orthodox) cannot cover the full story of global and historic Christian churches; examples with both ancient

---

[2]Roger E. Olson, Frank S. Mead, Samuel S. Hill, and Craig D. Atwood, *Handbook of Denominations in the United States*, 14th ed. (Nashville: Abingdon, 2018).

[3]Olson et al., *Handbook of Denominations*.

and very recent lineages include the non-Chalcedonian churches and the Independent African Churches. This landscape might be described as a beautiful diversity—a garden with many flowers—or as a heartbreaking disintegration of the body of Christ. There is probably truth in both descriptions, but it is undeniably the case that the contemporary church comprises a staggering breadth of difference.

No Christian faith, Protestant or otherwise, can be complacent about fragmentation and continue to dwell within the story of Scripture, wherein the unity of the people of God is both an assumption and a plea. We are a people called to "the unity of the Spirit in the bond of peace" (Eph 4:3) because "there is one body and one Spirit, just as you were called to the one hope of your calling, one Lord, one faith, one baptism" (Eph 4:4-5). More, our unity is mysteriously connected to the divine oneness, which is the most fundamental truth about all reality. Thus, our oneness—of body, Spirit, hope, Lord, faith, and baptism—is found in and founded on the "one God and Father of all, who is above all and through all and in all" (Eph 4:6). Would it be too audacious to suggest that Christian unity is meant to be a sign of monotheism, which is also to say, meant to be a pointer to the falseness of all idols? That Christian unity is also meant to bear witness to the same?

It is not only this passage from Ephesians that seems to suggest so. Jesus' prayer in John 17, rightly the most central and most cited passage in calls to Christian unity, makes that connection explicit. First, Jesus prays for unity, and he does so in stunning terms, asking that we "may be one" as he is one with the Father (Jn 17:11). If Christian unity is to look like divine unity, it becomes quite hard to define that unity, but surely we can say that it is to be real, serious, and relational. Jesus repeats this call, making explicit his inclusion not only of his first-century disciples but also of us: "I ask not only on behalf of these but also on behalf of those who believe in me through their word, that they may all be one. As you, Father, are in me and I am in you, may they also be in us, so that the world may believe that you have sent me. The glory that you have given me I have given them, so that they may be one, as we are one" (Jn 17:20-22). Our unity is "in" our incorporation into the triune life. It rests in the way that, through Jesus, in the power of the Spirit, we are "in" the one life of the one God. Here is the connection between unity and witness. Jesus prays that our oneness would reflect the divine oneness "so that the world may believe." Almost immediately, he repeats the thought: "I in them and you in me, that they may become completely one, so that the world may know that you have sent me and have loved them even as you have loved me" (Jn 17:23). There is no space here for Christians to be flippant about fragmentation. There is no space for us to ignore the reality and the seriousness of our call to be one, and if our oneness is meant to help the "world to know" Jesus, there is no room for our unity to be purely spiritual or invisible. If the world is meant to see, our unity must be visible.

Individualism and fragmentation are deep problems for Protestant faith, as are the problems with authority that so often come along with individualism and fragmentation. Protestantism insists that it is not the church but Scripture, as the very Word of God, that is the central site of authority for Christian faith. The problem, of course, is that Scripture is not easy to interpret, and having rejected the idea that the church is the trustworthy arbiter of right interpretation, we find ourselves in disagreement about matters of faith and practice. Traditional and individual interpretations compete, and sometimes those differences result in more fragmentation.

Authority is about the truth of who God is; it is about the nature and character of Jesus, the "author and perfecter of our faith" (Heb 12:2 NIV 1984). Here, the connection in English between *author* and *authority* helps us imagine an authority that is not authoritarian but is about the character of the author. Our author, Jesus, rightly bears authority because of who he is, very God, and Jesus also shows us the truth about the Father in the Spirit. Jesus-shaped authority is not about control and dominance; it is about love, which empties itself for our sake. We are concerned about right authority, then, not so we can control other Christians or the church but so we can tell truth about God, as revealed in the Son of the Father through the Spirit. Authority is about the goodness, truth, and beauty of God. Authority is about making it clear that the truth about reality is not that strong trumps weak. The truth about reality is love. I think here of the wrenching scene in the 1986 film *The Mission*, in which the character Father Gabriel (played by Jeremy Irons) rejects his fellow priest's plea for violence and goes to martyrdom with his people: "If might is right, then love has no place in the world. It may be so; it may be so. But I don't have the strength to live in a world like that." If we are to know God and be transformed to "bear the image" (1 Cor 15:49) of Jesus, no Christian faith, Protestant or otherwise, can give up on an account of true and accessible authority while continuing to dwell within the story of Scripture.

CONSENT AND PEACE

These typically modern problems—individualism, fragmentation, questions about authority—are not only problems. They come, too, with goods, a vision of life together in which we prize consent and peace. Those problems, then, are not unadulterated evil but offer solid goods to both theology and to politics. The story of a Christianity plagued by individualism, fragmentation, and lack of authoritative truth often centers Protestantism as responsible for these problems and assumes said problems are inherent to Protestant faith, inevitable results of *sola scriptura*. Told in this way, the story is about competing individual interpretations of Scripture leading to division and said division resulting in persecution, violence, and war. As Roman Catholic historian Brad Gregory recounts it, those competing interpretations of Scripture eventually result in protections for toleration and freedom of religion to prevent that violence, and Gregory reads that freedom of religion as "the renunciation" of "rulers' aspirations to promote a substantive moral community." Gregory assesses modernity as a bargain in favor of social stability over against social morality, realized through moving "to privatize religion and to distinguish it from public life, ideologically as well as institutionally, through politically protected rights to individual religious freedom."[4]

I'm suspicious of such grand stories, especially when those stories locate ruin in a particular figure or movement. Yes, Protestantism suffers from individualism, fragmentation, and related problems with authority, but I'm convinced neither that Protestantism is the cause of those problems nor that said

---

[4]Brad Gregory, *The Unintended Reformation: How a Religious Revolution Secularized Society* (Cambridge, MA: Harvard University Press, 2012), 216, 21.

problems are inbuilt to Protestantism in a way that makes Protestant faith untenable. These are characteristics not of Protestantism but of modernity, their sway over Protestant faith less the natural result of that faith than a sign of the times and their rise a phenomenon that began well before Luther's theses went up on that Wittenberg door and that would have ripened had Luther never existed. Protestantism did not cause modernity, nor did modernity cause Protestantism. Modernity was coming, Luther or no, and it touches every church tradition, including Protestant, Roman Catholic, and Eastern Orthodox, for good and for ill. It is the task of the whole church, including the Protestant, to learn from modernity where it is good and to challenge it, witnessing to another way, where it is evil. If we are coming now to dwell in the postmodern, the same will be true.

I'm not suggesting there is some pure and context-free thing called Protestantism but rather that Protestant faith is not confined to the sixteenth century and can grow into and thrive in other contexts, both learning from those contexts and challenging them to be continuously reformed by the gospel, just as that faith did in the past.[5] Rumors of individualism, fragmentation, and changes in understanding of authority were in the air in sixteenth-century Europe, had been brewing for some time, and continued to spread over the coming centuries. These challenges influenced and had to be grappled with by Roman

---

[5]Take, for example, this description of African Christianity from Lamin Sanneh: "African Christianity has not been a bitterly fought religion: there have been no ecclesiastical courts condemning unbelievers, heretics, and witches to death; no bloody battles of doctrine and polity; no territorial aggrandizement by churches; no jihads against infidels; no fatwas against women; no amputations, lynchings, ostracism, penalties, or public condemnations of doctrinal difference or dissent. The lines of Christian profession have not been etched in the blood of enemies." Sanneh, *Whose Religion Is Christianity: The Gospel Beyond the West* (Grand Rapids, MI: Eerdmans, 2003), 39.

Catholic faith going forward, as well as by Protestant faith. More so, individualism, fragmentation, and shifts in authority cannot be described only as problematic. They also come with gifts.

Gregory offers a gloomy assessment of the rise of social stability over against social morality. He sees a secular society with no room for shared morality. Fragmentation and the relativism that comes with it can make it difficult to find moral consensus, and Gregory is correct that toleration and religious freedom are at odds with the kind of moral community that expects the specific morality of one faith tradition to be adopted and practiced by a whole society; but it seems odd to suggest that the motive to end violence is not itself moral and, more, does not then create and sustain a certain kind of moral community, albeit one that prioritizes peace over unanimity and nonviolence over the authority to impose one moral tradition on a society as a whole. Protestant themes—anticlericalism, the call for believers to read Scripture for themselves, and the priesthood of all believers—are themes for a moral society that prizes consent and peace. Such a moral society has certainly been shaped by biblical morality, even as it refuses coercive efforts to require biblical morality as themselves unbiblical and immoral.

Let us take the Peace of Westphalia as an example. In 1658, it ended the Thirty Years' War by establishing toleration in the empire for Lutherans, Calvinists, and Roman Catholics, allowing private worship and liberty of conscience. The treaty calls for "a Christian and Universal Peace" to be "observ'd and cultivated with such a Sincerity and Zeal, that each Party shall endeavour to procure the Benefit, Honour and Advantage of the other; that thus on all sides they may see this Peace and

Friendship in the Roman Empire, and the Kingdom of France flourish, by entertaining a good and faithful Neighbourhood."[6] The language used here—*Christian, peace, good, faithful*—is both moral and theological. I am not suggesting that it is purely so. Politics is operating here at least as much as, probably more than, is theology. Most of the treaty is about the distribution of goods and power: who gets the churches; who gets the land, the palaces, the soldiers, the birthrights; who pays taxes and who receives; who sets the armies. When I note that the new toleration was as much about politics as it was religion, I am not making an original point, and the same is true for the violence that came before the toleration.[7]

A peace like that of Westphalia is far from morally faultless, and I'm not suggesting that such projects would be without negative consequences for either theology or politics. If the church itself is a broken thing, we shouldn't be surprised to find the peace of the state to be a broken thing as well. The lasting effects of the Peace of Westphalia were as much about national sovereignty as either faith or peace, and that is a project about which I'm less than hopeful.[8] What I am saying is just this: peace is a moral good, and a society that prioritizes peace shapes us in moral ways. Furthermore, the kind of moral society looked to in the hope of Westphalia for a "good and faithful Neighborhood" is a hope shaped by centuries of Christian faith and by long interaction with Scripture.

---

[6] "Treaty of Westphalia," 1648, Avalon Project: Documents in Law, History and Diplomacy at Yale Law School, https://avalon.law.yale.edu/17th_century/westphal.asp.

[7] William T. Cavanaugh, *The Myth of Religious Violence: Secular Ideology and the Roots of Modern Conflict* (Oxford: Oxford University Press, 2009).

[8] Again, Cavanaugh: "The myth of religious violence is inextricably bound up with the legitimation of the state and its use of violence" (*Myth of Religious Violence*, 124).

Said shaping is far from perfectly faithful, but a concept such as that of freedom of conscience does grow from a biblical view of the human being as created in the divine image, and the idea that faith comes by consent and not by force is a biblically shaped moral triumph over Constantinianism, crusade, and colonialism.[9] Inasmuch as individualism, fragmentation, and reframings of authority are bound together with hope for consent and for a vision of life together in peace, they bring goods for theology and for ecclesiology. In this book's final chapter, I will return to this second chapter of Ephesians, but I want to preview that by closing this section with a shout out to its theology of peace: "For he is our peace; in his flesh he has made both into one and has broken down the dividing wall, that is, the hostility between us" (Eph 2:14).

SOLA SCRIPTURA, WITH ALL ITS MESSINESS

Here is Brad Gregory's summary of the problem unleashed by Protestant confession of the unique authority of Scripture:

> Sola scriptura, even when supplemented by an insistence on the illuminating influence of the Holy Spirit, had created an unintended jungle of incompatible truth claims among those who rejected the Roman church, with no foreseeable likelihood of resolution. . . . Sola scriptura led to an open-ended proliferation of contested, competing doctrines among exegetical rivals, some of whom were

---

[9] A more subtle analysis, again from Cavanaugh: "I do not argue that these wars were not really about religion, but were really about politics or economics or culture. . . . To make such arguments is to assume that one can readily sort out what is 'religion' from what is 'politics' and so on in Reformation Europe. But these wars were themselves part of the process of creating those very distinctions. The creation of the modern state, in other words, was not simply the solution to the violence of the sixteenth and seventeenth centuries, but was itself implicated in the violence" (*Myth of Religious Violence*, 124).

demonstrating their willingness to die for their respective beliefs. Objectionably papist, merely human ecclesiastical tradition had simply been supplanted by objectionably subjective, merely human biblical interpreters.[10]

Oof. Gregory's pessimistic assessment is not his alone. I know many a convert from Protestantism to Roman Catholicism who has made that move for reasons like to Gregory's, and I know many Protestants who have dark nights, edging toward despair, over worries like these. But is this a full and fair assessment of the fruit of *sola scriptura*? Might there be ways to live with and from that Protestant principle that acknowledge the difficulties of interpreting Scripture while also finding there that which gives life? I believe there are.

Is the church essential, God's chosen way of working in the world, without which there is no Christian life? Or is the church so broken that it can and sometimes must be treated with the utmost suspicion? Any theology that takes the church seriously is bound to lean further in one direction or the other. The entirety of my theological training and all of my first instincts are in the first direction, so nobody will be more surprised than me if this book seems to lean in the other. But my wrestling with the church has brought me to this point; I see no way to claim the church as essential without at the same time being utterly wary of it. While this is too stark a way of putting the matter, if it comes down to a choice between trusting Scripture and trusting the church, I'm going to go with Scripture.[11] What if Scripture is not *quite* so hard to interpret as Gregory implies? And what if the difficulties of interpretation—which the whole church

---

[10]Gregory, *Unintended Reformation*, 89.
[11]Have you *seen* the church? See chapters above.

and not *sola* Protestants have spent the last several centuries facing—teach us something important about the nature of Scripture, the nature of the God whose Word that Scripture is, and the nature of the life that God would have us seek together in faithfulness?

Let's begin with the second question. What does interpretive complexity teach us? What kind of Scriptures do we have, and what does that suggest about the God we know through these words? Christian faith teaches that the Scriptures are inspired by the Spirit's work in and with multiple human authors, that we receive those texts as canon, and that we rely on the illuminating power of the Spirit to read that canon well. The canon has a center, about which we can discern enough family resemblance among interpretations to be able to recognize it or at least to object when we fail to do so. In my judgment, that center is reliably identified in the early ecumenical creeds, with a Protestant center extending past the creeds to *sola scriptura* and *sola gratia*. That many will be unsatisfied with my personal assessment of the center does not mean no center exists. That a thing is hard to see may say more about the viewer than the thing we are trying to view. As to the edges of the canon, we are free to a diversity of interpretations, particularly as those are sensitive to context, and more importantly, we are free to the task of being the kind of body in which that diversity may flourish. *These* Scriptures, of *this* nature, testify to a God who chooses to work among us in this peculiar way, to make Godself known here, and so invites us into relationship, community, freedom, and mystery and not into interpretive certainty. As a sign in my sister-in-law's kitchen has it: "God bless this beautiful mess."

Consider the nature of the Scriptures as canon. What does it mean that we receive Scripture as a diverse collection of texts, written over multiple centuries through the Spirit's work with and in multiple human authors? Perhaps it means that those Scriptures are best read as an invitation to relationship with the God of the canonical community and not as a set of propositions over which we hope to achieve interpretive mastery.[12] Here I have learned from the late Roman Catholic theologian Lamin Sanneh. Born in the Gambia, Sanneh converted from Islam to Christianity. His work connects Scripture as canon and as a translated medium to the good of Christian plurality around the world. Sanneh contrasts the nature of Christian Scripture as canon with a Muslim doctrine of Scripture, which understands the Qur'an to have been received by dictation, by one prophet, in one time and place. While the Qur'an cannot be translated and retain its status as Scripture (translations being understood as paraphrases but not as Scripture itself), the Christian canon positively *requires* translation, as it already, in its original languages, encompasses more than one language, community, and culture. Christian Scripture *by its very nature* is translatable, and biblical translation, Sanneh argues, shows us the vernacular character of Christian faith. Thus, says Sanneh, the "Bible helped engender an anti-elitist culture of open access, with a bias toward people of low social origins."[13] Again:

> The fact of Christianity being a translated, and translating, religion places God at the center of the universe of cultures, implying free coequality among cultures and a necessary relativizing of languages vis-à-vis the truth of God.

---

[12]By "canonical community" I mean the community that claims these texts as canon.
[13]Sanneh, *Whose Religion Is Christianity*, 118.

No culture is so advanced and so superior that it can claim exclusive access or advantage to the truth of God, and none so marginal or inferior that it can be excluded.[14]

Remarkably, "Bible translation does not so much destroy the power of religion as put that power into the hands of ordinary people, yes, especially women and children."[15]

Biblical inspiration via dictation would be quite neat and tidy, but the nature of the Christian canon displays that such cannot be the way the Spirit acted in the lives of the human authors of Scripture. Their books preserve their personalities, writing styles, quirks, and varied contextual and communal needs. Dictation would presumably have flattened those differences, and the fact that difference stands within Scripture itself is testimony to God's chosen way of working in the world and in human lives. I had a seminary professor who said that the canon includes four Gospels because "God loves peace." Against the Marcionite move to narrow the canon (which would, among other things, have cut things down to just one Gospel), the recognized Christian canon is generous and expansive. It invites us to live with and to learn from diverse takes on our one shared story. As Sanneh has it, "Christianity is not intrinsically a religion of cultural uniformity, and . . . it has demonstrated that empirically by reflecting the tremendous diversity and dynamism of the peoples of the world."[16] The fact of canonicity invites us to live with difference in honest conversation and ongoing loving community, not to excise that difference. It invites us to welcome human diversity and to give up on trying to

---

[14]Sanneh, *Whose Religion Is Christianity*, 105.
[15]Sanneh, *Whose Religion Is Christianity*, 117.
[16]Sanneh, *Whose Religion Is Christianity*, 130-31.

grasp or tame God in favor of seeking relationship with the one who is the God of all four Gospels and of the whole messy canonical community. It invites us to a moral community of consent and peace.

However, too much Protestant theology has sought propositional clarity over personal knowledge of God, and that search is often inappropriate to the nature of Scripture itself.[17] It is also the case that Protestant theology contains resources to shift us away from hope for interpretive mastery and toward vital, personal relationship with the God of the Scriptures. Here I will largely follow Phillip Cary, who argues that attempts at propositional certainty have been a painful legacy of the Reformation.[18] The story goes, loosely, like this: Reformers framed the Protestant project as a contest over the correct reading of Scripture, thus elevating interpretive certainty as the goal of recognizing Scripture as the ultimate authority for Christian faith and life. Protestants claimed that Protestant readings were the correct and certain readings of Scripture. Per Cary:

> Protestant theologians in fact undertook to prove that the Bible and its promises could not possibly be read contrary to the way Protestants read it—as if faith in God's promises were not possible until the theologians on our side proved without a doubt that the theologians on their side misunderstood the meaning of Scripture. This is a subtle but

---

[17] Phillip Cary, *The Meaning of Protestant Theology: Luther, Augustine, and the Gospel That Gives Us Christ* (Grand Rapids, MI: Baker Academic, 2019).

[18] It seems more likely to me that Luther here is not the *source* of the trouble but is instead one representative—albeit an important one—of a kind of trouble that was brewing in the wider consciousness of late medieval Europe, a trouble that infected both the Protestant and Catholic Reformations and bloomed more fully in the post-Reformation world, both Protestant and Roman Catholic.

terrible mistake, for it meant putting faith not in the word of God alone but also in the correctness of our interpretation, and it had very bad consequences in the long run.[19]

These attempts at proof of correct doctrine were then "solidified in institutionalized claims of theological certainty that fared very badly against the rise of modern biblical scholarship." On Cary's account, that goal of theological certainty became impossible with three major developments; first, seventeenth-century pluralism showed that competing truth claims can be irreconcilable; second, the rise of an eighteenth-century "neutral, secularized conception of 'reason'" turned us to science in our hopes for certainty; and third, nineteenth-century biblical scholarship treated Scripture as an object for supposedly neutral, scientific inquiry. So, Cary concludes, that which "had seemed transparent and perspicuous in the sixteenth century came to seem opaque and obscure in the nineteenth century, requiring a different kind of interpretation from that practiced in the church."[20]

Cary doesn't leave us there. His account would revitalize a Protestant doctrine of Scripture, asking us to ground our reading in the gospel of Jesus Christ. Human knowledge is personal, and when considering faith in Jesus, the way we know will have to be the way we know another person. That is, said knowledge is less proposition and more relationship.[21] Reading Scripture in faith, says Cary, "rests on the truth of another person, his faithfulness in keeping his word. Its basis is not our

---

[19]Cary, *Meaning of Protestant Theology*, 208.

[20]Cary, *Meaning of Protestant Theology*, 207, 216, 219.

[21]See also Esther Lightcap Meek, *Longing to Know: The Philosophy of Knowledge for Ordinary People* (Grand Rapids, MI: Brazos, 2003), and *Loving to Know: Covenant Epistemology* (Eugene, OR: Cascade, 2011).

ability to prove or see or establish scientifically the truth to which we cling, yet it does have a solid basis because God is indeed true to his word." This is not a rejection of the Protestant principle of Scripture alone but a reclaiming of that principle in a way that makes better sense of the way humans know and of the nature of the biblical text itself. Again, from Cary: "The only lasting foundation is Scripture itself, to which Christian theology must constantly return as it keeps learning the Gospel afresh, in the conviction that the Scriptural witness to Jesus Christ continues to have something to say to the church in every era, because the church is the same community that the Scriptures have been addressing all along."[22]

In calling us to the person Jesus, Scripture invites us to live with difference, embracing the beauty of a plurality gathered around the one Lord. The one community of the Scriptures is the unified diversity of the Revelator's "great multitude that no one could count, from every nation, from all tribes and peoples and languages, standing before the throne and before the Lamb, robed in white, with palm branches in their hands" (Rev 7:9). Gregory's account of the contemporary world sees only a "hyperpluralism of religious and secular commitments, not any shared or even convergent view about what 'we' think is true or right or good."[23] Yet, where Gregory sees only fragmentation and dissolution, Sanneh sees "Christian pluralism" as "not just a matter of regrettable doctrinal splits and ecclesiastical fragmentation, but rather of variety and diversity within each church tradition."[24]

---

[22]Cary, *Meaning of Protestant Theology*, 227, 225.
[23]Gregory, *Unintended Reformation*, 11.
[24]Sanneh, *Whose Religion Is Christianity*, 130.

A peaceful pluralism is not absent an account of the right and the good, but that account, on its own internal grounds, will require that the right and the good come with respect for the freedom and dignity of persons as invited —never coerced—to enter that good. If rejecting one authorized interpretation of Scripture comes with fragmentation, it also comes with freedom. The right and the good cannot be the right and the good if they are forced, and conscience and consent—even when they are treated as secular goods—could not have been recognized as good without a societal imagination shaped by the canonical Scriptures. Sanneh also makes this connection, identifying "the mental habits of Christendom" as those that "predispose us to look for one essence of the faith, with a corresponding global political structure as safeguard." In contrast, "world Christianity challenges us to pay attention to the dynamic power of the gospel and to the open-ended character of communities of faith."[25] Consider these two accounts of the right and the good, both formed by the biblical witness to freedom and consent as the properly human ways in which humans may relate to God. The first is from Sanneh (1942–2019), world Christian and Roman Catholic, the second from Elisha Williams (1694–1755), Congregationalist and Protestant.

> It is therefore not fatal to faith that people choose and decide freely, however great the risk of human entanglement; otherwise faith would cease to be what it is. No one can be saved against his or her will, though the will, prone to willfulness, is not an end in itself. Conversion is not to people, to techniques, or even to theories, but to

---

[25]Sanneh, *Whose Religion Is Christianity*, 35.

God in whom is our true freedom, and the proof of that is in the knowledge and love God grants.[26]

Every man has an equal right to follow the dictates of his own conscience in the affairs of religion. Every one is under an indispensable obligation to search the scripture for himself (which contains the whole of it) and to make the best use of it he can for his own information in the will of GOD, the nature and duties of Christianity. And as every Christian is so bound; so he has an unalienable right to judge of the sense and meaning of it, and to follow his judgment wherever it leads him; even an equal right with any rulers be they civil or ecclesiastical.[27]

Here, the Congregationalist Protestant and the Roman Catholic world Christian point together to the good God of freedom. This description is not by itself adequate for ecclesial life, but the goods attached to it are not to be rejected. Protestantism needs to hold these goods while also reading Scripture together with the community, learning from the church spread across time and space.

On Williams's diagnosis, "No action is a religious action without understanding and choice in the agent."[28] If there is truth in this account, then Protestantism needs to revive a doctrine now firmly out of fashion, that of the perspicuity of Scripture (the claim that Scripture is clear and understandable, at least in its central meaning). I am not suggesting that the

---

[26]Sanneh, *Whose Religion Is Christianity*, 56.

[27]Elisha Williams, "The Essential Rights and Liberties of Protestants: A Seasonable Plea for the Liberty of Conscience, and the Right of Private Judgment, in Matters of Religion" (Boston: S. Kneeland and T. Green, 1744), reproduced in *Individualism: A Reader*, ed. George H. Smith and Marilyn Moore (N.p.: Libertarianism.org Press, 2015), 175.

[28]Williams, "Essential Rights and Liberties," 176.

goods of diversity, consent, and peace require giving up on unity or truth. Many tribes are gathered around the one throne of the one Lamb. In Daniela C. Augustine's expressive prose:

> Pentecost's polyglotic summoning of all nations under heaven by the proclamation of the Good News of God in their ethnic tongue is an in-breaking of the eschata and a prophetic foretaste of all ethnicities' joined destiny in Christ. We catch a glimpse of this glorious telos in the magnificent vision of redeemed humanity articulated in the book of Revelation. The vision crescendos into a breathtaking narrative of the worshiping multitude "standing before the throne" of God and the Lamb (Rev. 7:9) This Colossal human mass that no eye can count moves in sacramental singularity of purpose and desire, worshiping its Redeemer, washed in His blood, sanctified by His Spirit. Yet, here John sees represented every tongue and every nation of the world. They are distinctly identifiable; they have not lost their ethnographic uniqueness in that redeemed oneness. Their white robes point to the common experience of redemption and sanctification. The multitude is one with the Savior. Yet, they stand before God not only as Christ's one Body but also as persons, nations and cultures, for He has preserved diversity within oneness.[29]

What if disagreement over the meaning of Scripture is less chaotic than it is often made out to be? I promise I am not as naive as you may well have just decided that I am. I'm aware of the facts of variant readings, from readings of specific biblical

---

[29]Daniela C. Augustine, *Pentecost, Hospitality, and Transfiguration: Toward a Spirit-Inspired Vision of Social Transformation* (Cleveland, TN: CPT Press, 2012), 133. Thanks to Abby Anderson for drawing my attention to this quotation.

passages to readings of the Bible as a whole, and I am also aware of the history attached to those different readings. But, if Cary is right, if Scripture is more relational and less propositional, more gospel and less doing-the-work-of-interpretive-certainty, then I do believe—often by faith and not by sight—that Scripture reveals the truth of Christian faith, the truth about God and humans, the meaning of life, the universe, and everything.

To claim that Scripture is perspicacious is to claim that it can be understood and, more importantly, can be lived out in faith. Let me offer a few stories about how Scripture makes itself clear. Slaveholders in the American South understood, at the gut level, enough about the perspicuity of Scripture to decide to work actively against it. Hence the action of slaveholders to withhold the fullness of the Scriptures from the people they enslaved.[30] While slaveholders argued in public that the clear meaning of Scripture supported their practice of slaveholding, their actions to restrict Black people from access to the Scriptures make another argument entirely. And—praise to the one who revealed the Word to us—when those enslaved people did get access to Scripture, sometimes doing so while incurring the risk of grave personal danger, they did read there, rightly, the gospel story and the implications of that story for the freedom of all human beings.

One of my theology teachers, the late ecumenical and Methodist theologian Geoffrey Wainwright, would tell a story in class when he introduced the ecumenical nature of the creeds. His story went something like this:[31] He sat in a meeting for the

---

[30]Henry Louis Gates Jr., *The Black Church: This Is Our Story, This Is Our Song* (New York: Penguin, 2021), chap. 1, Kindle.

[31]I'm reconstructing from memory what he was reconstructing from memory. This is a story, not history, though, because I knew the person Geoffrey Wainwright, I have full confidence that it points faithfully to history.

World Council of Churches. The question at debate was whether the historic creeds should serve as a standard for that body. Some Western representatives turned to representatives from the Majority World and said, "Surely, you wouldn't want us to use the creeds? They're poisoned by Greek thought." But the representatives from Africa, Asia, and Latin America said, "That may be, but what the creeds describe is what we believe."

Now, I'm deeply wary of North American and European theologians mustering non-Western voices in favor of "our" arguments, whatever side "we" may be on, but I do think this story points to a deep truth about the clarity of Scripture. The creeds, in my judgment, are the best summary statements of the center of Scripture that we have. If I'm at all right about the faithfulness of those summaries, then it is not surprising that Christians who are outside creedal traditions but inside biblical traditions should recognize those creeds as faithful articulations of biblical faith. Inasmuch as the creeds are faithful to Scripture, recognizable to Christians who may be noncreedal and who have been formed in contexts very different from those in which the creeds were formed, the perspicuity of Scripture is evident.

These stories don't offer an obvious account of perspicuity. They require an ecclesial and historical account of perspicuity. Slaveholders had to test their accounts of Scripture against those of White and Black abolitionists. Delegates to the World Council of Churches had to sit together, around a table, representing the church bodies from which they came. Scripture is not clear without interpretation. Scripture is not Scripture without illumination, and Protestant theologies need not attempt to produce theology out of nothing; we have good, ecclesial reasons to claim unity with the church across the centuries and the church across the continents.

Nor are we bereft of helpful interpretive aids. There are matters in Scripture that are relatively central and relatively clear (creedal matters, for instance), and there are matters in Scripture that are less central and less clear. Lack of total perspicuity does not mean we have no understanding; in fact, that lack of totality itself testifies to understanding the text well enough to sort the central from the peripheral. Lack of propositional certainty is not a lack of meeting the Lord of the gospel. The priority of Scripture does not require that we attempt interpretation without the tradition of the church. In fact, the priority of Scripture might well require just that sort of interpretation, as the human voices in Scripture are themselves an interpretative community that invite us to enter into and extend that community of interpretation.[32] So, says Cary, "Renewal of the meaning of Protestant theology today requires bringing the focus back to the Gospel promise that gives us Christ, which also means returning to the shared authorities of the Christian tradition and giving up the kind of claims to theological certainty that emerged in the course of sixteenth-century polemics."[33] Perspicuity is personal, not propositional. What we meet clearly in Scripture is not a series of factual statements; we meet a person, Jesus Christ, the only Son of the Father, one with us and one with God in the Spirit. We know Jesus as persons know persons, not primarily as a set of facts but as a character, one whom we learn—from Scripture—to be trustworthy.[34]

---

[32]Ellen Davis, "Critical Traditioning: Seeking an Inner Biblical Hermeneutic," *Anglican Theological Review* 82, no. 4 (September 2000): 733-51.

[33]Cary, *Meaning of Protestant Theology*, 216.

[34]See again Meek, *Longing to Know* and *Loving to Know*.

I find an unlikely lesson in perspicuity in the fiction of Margaret Atwood, a master of writing dystopian worlds. Several of her shattered worlds feature characters and communities distorting Scripture for their own power and purposes. Her best-known work is *The Handmaid's Tale*, wherein a totalitarian and hyperpatriarchal theocracy known as Gilead has overthrown the government of the United States and uses brutal measures to control women's bodies and exploit their reproductive capacities. Gilead puts tight controls on the reading of Scripture, including forbidding women to read. Atwood has a knack for rendering power-mongering in the name of religion, and though Gilead is fictional, it is also recognizable and true enough to send a shiver through readers.

Yet, Atwood has an instinct that the Scriptures may yet speak for themselves, may yet speak against the powers and principalities. It matters that the words are accessible, and it matters who the reader is. In her more recent novel, *The Testaments*, we find ourselves further into the history of Gilead. A central character is a young woman who has managed to avoid forced marriage to train as an "Aunt," a woman used by the theocracy to discipline and control other women. In Gilead, the Aunts are an exception to the rule banning women from reading. Her new permission to read Scripture for herself shakes the young woman: "The first of my inner storms came about when . . . I was finally granted reading access to the full Bible. Our Bibles were kept locked up, as elsewhere in Gilead: only those of strong mind and steadfast character could be trusted with them, and that ruled out women, except for the Aunts."[35] It matters

---

[35] Margaret Atwood, *The Testaments* (New York: Anchor, 2020), Kindle.

who does the reading, be it totalitarian power monger or vulnerable girl. Our character is excited to read the Bible for the first time, but the actual reading upsets her world.

> Up until that time I had not seriously doubted the rightness and especially the truthfulness of Gilead's theology. If I'd failed at perfection, I'd concluded that the fault was mine. But as I discovered what had been changed by Gilead, what had been added, and what had been omitted, I feared I might lose my faith. If you've never had a faith, you will not understand what that means. You feel as if your best friend is dying; that everything that defined you is being burned away; that you'll be left all alone. You feel exiled, as if you are lost in a dark wood.[36]

There we have it: a doctrine of perspicuity. Reading the Bible reveals that "you could believe in Gilead or you could believe in God, but not both."[37]

---

[36]Atwood, *Testaments*, 303.
[37]Atwood, *Testaments*, 304.

SIX

THE PECULIAR STRENGTHS
OF PROTESTANTISM

IMAGINE YOU ARE AT A FAMILY GATHERING—I won't tell you whether it's my side of the family or my husband's—and Contrarian Uncle, a skeptic, is enjoying lobbing contrarian arguments at his Christian family members. He says, "You're Christians because you were born in Christian families, in a mostly Christian country. If you'd been born in Pakistan, you'd probably be Muslim."

Contrarian Uncle settles back into the sofa, a satisfied smile on his face, convinced he's clinched his argument against Christian faith by making it clear that said faith was never a purely individual decision, chosen rationally after having considered all other options. Instead, that faith's legibility and his family's deluded clinging to it are embedded in context and culture.

I don't think I'm going to convince Contrarian Uncle, but I'm not particularly impressed by his argument, as I don't think that embeddedness in context and culture are strikes against faith. I think they're good things, as I'm persuaded that God loves contexts and cultures and works in the particularities of them. I'm also not persuaded that faith should be a purely rational choice, having been made after considering all the options, because I don't think that's a true account of the ways humans come to know and to love. Contrarian Uncle is also unaware of how culturally embedded his own criteria of individually chosen rationality are. All of that is to say, when I'm faced with the question, "Why stay Protestant?" I'm tempted to say, "Because I was born that way."

LOVING HOME, THE HISTORIC CHURCH

There's something to rooting where one was planted, to doing the work of loving home, even though—especially though?—one didn't choose that home. Please hear me; I'm not suggesting that changing Christian traditions is a bad thing or that it should never be done. One can absolutely move into a new home, and there are all kinds of good reasons to do so. Perhaps you need more space, or your children have moved and you want to be near them. Perhaps you're floored by the beauty of that new place you've found, with its soaring views or cozy kitchen table by the fireplace. I'm not condemning moving house, and when a first home has been violent or deceptive, inhospitable or bare, then it's not just that one *may* move; in such cases, moving may become necessary to health and to truth telling, and I'd pray that we find the courage to do so.

There are very good reasons to leave a home, but when one *can* stay, there are also good reasons to plant oneself firmly in that home place. I'm not Roman Catholic or Eastern Orthodox in part because I'm trying to learn to love my home. Day after day, year after year, being faithful to that home in all its beauty and strangeness and failure teaches me something about the God who is faithful to us and who ultimately *is* our home.

In their book *The Home of God*, Miroslav Volf and Ryan McAnnally-Linz claim the metaphor of home as central to understanding God's work in the world. In doing so, they give us a gift: a theology for the world, a theology of worldly character. Their theology is one in which this world is becoming God's true home. It is one in which incarnation "underscores the significance of the home's materiality and shows that the presence of God in the world in no way detracts from its worldliness but brings the world in its worldliness to fulfillment." It is a theology in which our end is good work in the world that is God's home, wherein "All that remains is thirsting after more of just that world—more of God and the world in their distinction and unity—and therefore maintaining and enhancing it."[1] Just this worldliness, I believe, is a vital center of Christian theology because it is so deeply about Jesus.

To say that I am Protestant because Protestantism is my home is a way of acknowledging the historicity of the church. Church isn't something one chooses in a vacuum. The choice for church is made in the ongoing historical concreteness of real life in the real world. I'm Protestant because my people were Protestant. I know more of the history on my dad's side of the family; his people came to the Midwest from Germany. Generations back, we can find records of the Lutherans in an unbroken line, a line that extends across the Atlantic to that now barely remembered German home. There's some evidence—admittedly vague— that my people were Lutherans going as far back as the

---

[1] Miroslav Volf and Ryan McAnnally-Linz, *The Home of God: A Brief Story of Everything* (Grand Rapids, MI: Brazos, 2022), 90, 219.

Reformation. An ancestor who was executed as a witch was also mother to many Lutheran pastors. Before they were Lutherans, of course, they were Roman Catholics, and before that they were pagans. History connects me to my dad, to his dad, to families on boats to America, to a little church in a little German town, to the clergy sons of a witch, to, perhaps, converts to Christianity in the eighth century. I'm not romanticizing this. Son of those Lutherans and a very Methodist mother, whatever my dad's experiences with this Protestant history were, he has now converted to Roman Catholicism. I'm not romanticizing, but I am saying this history matters. My Protestant bones are descended from generations of Protestant bones. The same is true for the Protestant bones of the brand-new Christian convert at Baptist church camp or Anglican small group or Methodist altar call; the Protestant church, no less than any other church, is part and parcel of the historic church of Jesus.

GRATIA

We had to get here eventually. It would be odd to write about being Protestant without turning to that central doctrine: justification by faith alone, through grace alone, in Christ alone. Here we Protestants stand; once for all, we impress on the church the freedom and the life-giving nature of divine grace. In the tradition of Augustine, we entreat all believers to trust in the gift-giving God: "Why do you try to stand in your own strength and fail? Cast yourself upon God and have no fear. He will not shrink away and let you fall. Cast yourself upon him without fear, for he will welcome you and cure you of your ills."[2] With Luther, we invite the church to rest in the faith that

---

[2]Augustine, *Confessions*, trans. Maria Boulding (New York: Vintage, 1998), 8.11.

unites the soul with Christ as a bride is united with her bridegroom. By this mystery, as the Apostle teaches, Christ and the soul become one flesh. . . . Accordingly the believing soul can boast of and glory in whatever Christ has as though it were its own, and whatever the soul has Christ claims as his own . . . for if Christ is a bridegroom, he must take upon himself the things which are his bride's and bestow upon her the things that are his. If he gives her his body and very self, how shall he not give her all that is his? And if he takes the body of the bride, how shall he not take all that is hers?[3]

We revel in that marvelous exchange, in which Christ takes all that is ours, including our sin, and graces us with all that is his, including his righteousness.

I would never claim that Protestants have sole access or even privileged access to the gospel of grace, but perhaps Protestants exist to highlight that grace, to remind ourselves and our fellow gospel Christians—in Roman Catholic and Eastern Orthodox and all other Christian traditions—that we live by gift and die in gift and will rise again one day as gift of the graciousness of Christ our Lord. This book is not the place to attempt a full account of justification by grace, but I will briefly highlight some aspects of that Protestant witness, and I'll point to some ways the conversation might continue to give life to the church.

Alister McGrath provides an account of Protestantism on the doctrine of justification by grace, which is for us a good starting point for thinking about how Protestants have

---

[3]Martin Luther, "The Freedom of a Christian," in *Luther's Works*, American ed. (Philadelphia: Fortress, 1957), 31:356.

historically talked of grace.[4] His account circles around three key teachings. First, Protestant theology maintains a difference between justification (in which we are declared righteous in Christ) and sanctification (in which we are transformed and become Christlike). Distinguishing between the two highlights that sanctification is not prerequisite to or cause of justification. All of life in Christ is a gift of grace. Second, Protestant theology teaches that Christ's righteousness is *imputed* to us, making justification a forensic act. God declares our legal status: righteous. God's declaration is not based on anything we have done but on Christ alone. This claim is also meant to emphasize that salvation is by divine grace and not by human effort. Finally, according to McGrath, Protestant theology identifies the righteousness by which we are justified as the "alien" righteousness of Jesus Christ. That righteousness is alien because it is not our own. It comes to us as a gift, from outside us, from Jesus. Again, the cause of justification is Jesus and not us, grace and not works, God's goodness and not our merit.

I do not reject McGrath's account. It is valuable, and it describes what I too profess as a clear articulation of Protestant reception and interpretation of the Augustinian tradition, which magnifies the gratuity of grace. At the same time, this kind of account can raise concern. While mapping a Protestant way of preaching grace, it can become casuistic; these concepts have too often been used for recrimination, cut off from the living root of faith. The terms here are also more common in certain swaths of Protestantism; as a lifelong Christian in the Wesleyan strain of Protestantism, I had never, not once, heard

---

[4]Alister McGrath, *Iustitia Dei: A History of the Christian Doctrine of Justification*, 2nd ed. (Cambridge: Cambridge University Press, 1998), 212.

most of this vocabulary until I was well into my doctoral studies in theology. This doesn't mean I was unacquainted with the concepts of grace in McGrath's account, but I had not heard the word *imputation*. McGrath's account is teeming with technical language, much of it coined in polemical context. We have not only the well-known and ecumenical terms *justification* and *sanctification* but also *imputed, forensic,* and *alien righteousness*.

This way of talking is very good at delineating the priority of grace, but as a language of lived faith it is a far cry from Luther's personal, relational invocation of Christ and the soul becoming one flesh. As a way of talking about justification, it is less typical of Protestantism as a whole and more so of the Continental Protestant tradition. Unfortunately, this language has also been used for gatekeeping, as if those wielding these terms can reliably assess whether a group or a person is Protestant enough.[5]

Theological traditions are rather like persons; often, their greatest strength is also their greatest weakness.[6] (My own stubbornness, perhaps?) If Protestantism exists to celebrate divine grace, it is also the case that certain Protestant ways of doing so correlate with characteristic problems. To distinguish justification from sanctification is right and good until that distinction becomes a rift, and we begin to practice discipleship as if the point were getting people to recite formulaic prayers and not the personal God in whom we are being transformed in faithfulness to Jesus Christ for the sake of the world God loves. To say that righteousness is imputed (or declared or reckoned) to us, even while true righteousness is alien to our being, can free us from Sisyphean

---

[5]I once taught a class about John Wesley with a rather Reformed-leaning group of students, and they spent the whole semester trying to determine whether Wesley really believed in imputed righteousness. He does, y'all. But also imparted.

[6]Whether more like persons than are corporations, I will leave to the reader to judge.

struggles to merit salvation and help us to recognize gift and love for what they are. This is so until we forget that the story of Jesus offers us righteousness both imputed and imparted, both declared our own and truly transforming us in Christlikeness.

When a tradition's strength is also its weakness, it becomes easy for adherents to that tradition to grow frustrated with that weakness and offer much criticism without also continuing to see its strength. But that doesn't have to be the case. We don't have to jettison salvation by grace to see the bigger gospel picture. I'm Protestant enough to think that if we do throw justification by grace overboard, we'll be left unable to see or to embrace that bigger gospel, but the gospel is not just justification by grace. The gospel is deep and wide. I'm happy to see justification by grace—centered on the life, death, and resurrection of Jesus—as the beating heart of the gospel, without which the limbs will not be able to thrive and serve.

My hope for the future of theology around the doctrine of justification is that we might continue in the Protestant tradition, highlighting the graciousness of God with Protestant technical language but also highlighting that graciousness even more by acknowledging the mysteries and surprises inherent in the work of God we point toward when we use words such as *imputation*. The "new perspective" on Paul reminds us of the Jewishness of Jesus and that the grace of the Old Testament is continuous with the grace of the New Testament. The gracious character of the one God does not change, and that grace calls us to a new way of life for the sake of the world.

With these insights in mind, I might suggest that the story of grace is not best told by confining it to a technical framework. (Though I do think that technical framework remains valuable and helps us tell the story of grace as it has been claimed through the centuries of the church.) The story of grace needs also to be told as the story of God's work for God's people, the story of Israel and the church called out from the world for the sake of the world. The story of grace recounts the faithfulness of Jesus Christ, in whom our trust is safely placed, in whom we may share the status of children and heirs.

OUTSIDE US, ALL BELIEVERS, AND THE GOSPEL OF GRACE

At the end of the day, I stay Protestant because I need God. I don't need another broken creature. I need the holy and righteous Creator. The church is good, and our good God chooses to work within it, but the church is not God, nor can church teaching be identified as the Word of God without grave risk of error and idolatry. I need that Protestant "external Word," a concept that reminds us of our need for the only one who is God, who comes to us from outside our realm of finitude and sin. I need to be addressed from outside human brokenness and human messes. I need to be transformed by the Word made flesh, the only one who is both fully God and fully human and so comes to us from the outside—*extra nos*—and from the inside—incarnate—because he loves us. I need union with the divine. Thank God the choice is not so simple, but if forced to a choice between the church and the Scriptures, I'm going to choose Scripture, in which I trust as the Word of the God, for us, from outside us. I feel the weight of centuries of Protestant claims made on 1 Timothy 2:5-6:

> There is one God;
>> there is also one mediator between God
>>> and humankind,

Christ Jesus, himself human,
   who gave himself a ransom for all.

We need the only one who is outside us, the only eternal, transcendent God. More, we need the wonderful and paradoxical good news that said God comes to us most intimately, the Word made flesh, so that our flesh might be drawn into the very life of God.

While I firmly believe in the unity of the baptismal font and the Lord's table (more on that in the next chapter), I'm also persuaded by classic Protestant theology in its concern that Roman Catholic and Eastern Orthodox theologies can take sacrament, which truly is outside us, and weld it so tightly to the authority of a human church that we are in danger of missing the dramatic external Word, the gospel of grace, which is offered in water, bread, and cup. This does *not* require opting for a symbolic account of the sacraments and rejecting the fleshy realism of what God does in material things. From almost the beginning, Protestantism has been a space with room for both symbolic and realist accounts of sacrament. The people in the room haven't always been happy with each other, but still there they are, all of them Protestant. Protestant sacramentology is capacious enough for Zwingli's symbolism and Luther's physicalism. When Zwingli insisted that the bread and wine were symbols, he feared that to call them otherwise would tempt us to magical thinking about the table and the font, which would have us turn the sacraments into works we can perform to earn favor with God. When Luther insisted that the bread and cup were true and physical body and blood, he feared that anything less would turn the sacraments into works we must perform by feeling or understanding the symbols. What, then, makes Protestant sacramentology distinctly Protestant? The answer is the gospel of grace. Sacrament is grace, not work. I don't need a rite, says Zwingli; I need Jesus. So says Luther: I don't need a symbol; I need Jesus.

As is the case with Protestant doctrines of Scripture, Protestant sacramentology must reject clericalism and hierarchical church control of the means of grace. Here Protestant insistence on the priesthood of all believers is part and parcel with the gospel of grace:

> Come to him, a living stone, though rejected by mortals yet chosen and precious in God's sight, and like living stones let yourselves be built into a spiritual house, to be a holy priesthood, to offer spiritual sacrifices acceptable to God through Jesus Christ. For it stands in scripture:
> "See, I am laying in Zion a stone,
>   a cornerstone chosen and precious,
> and whoever believes in him will not be put to shame."
> . . . But you are a chosen people, a royal priesthood, a holy nation, God's own people, in order that you may proclaim the excellence of him who called you out of darkness into his marvelous light. (1 Pet 2:4-6, 9)

The egalitarian impulse built into Protestant faith is the impulse of the gospel of grace. The grace by which Israel is Israel is the grace by which the church is the church. The church of grace is not one of hierarchy and authoritarian rule but one in which each and all are called to God's holy priesthood. When Protestant faith insists there is no mediator between humans and God but Christ alone, the result does not have to be—and shouldn't be—a bare individualism, but the result does require that each living stone in God's house stands in radical equality with every other. None is other than a stone supported by Christ the cornerstone. Here the priesthood of all believers should claim the fruiting of the gracious truth that every human is created in the image of God, women alongside men. Folks from every tribe and tongue and nation are called to share the good news. Grace rejects patriarchy, misogyny, racism, nationalism, and the politics of power.

I'm not suggesting that only Protestants can participate in that rejection, nor that all Protestant traditions have lived this out, but it's no coincidence that it is in Protestant churches that we have seen revival of the early church practice of opening leadership roles to women. Though Protestant churches vary widely in how far they have embraced that opening, credibly Protestant sacramentology cannot allow the Roman Catholic argument that priests must be male in order to represent Christ with their male bodies.[7] (Of course, some Protestants have other reasons for excluding women from leadership, but those are based in exegetical arguments, not a sacramental theology of priesthood that excludes the "all believers.") Protestant theology cannot entertain turning priest into mediator. Instead, the sacraments are themselves a visible word from outside us, no church standing between us and the grace of God. While life after the Reformation certainly included gains and losses for women on both Protestant and Roman Catholic sides of the divide, it is instructive to see female Reformers appealing to the external Word of God, received through Scripture, as the basis of their authority to speak and write.

---

[7] Of course, some Anglo-Catholics do admit such an idea, but while I'm sympathetic to Anglo-Catholicism in many ways, I'm calling this one out of Protestant bounds.

It is critical to understand that the relatively few women we know of who actively participated in theological discussions in the Reformation were just as passionately committed to the principle of sola scriptura as were their male counterparts. For these female writers, the only authority that ultimately mattered was that of God, as expressed through Scripture. Thus, for female writers, the Bible . . . provided final and absolute justification for dismissing secular (male) authorities who were acting contrary to the will of God . . . (as defined by the female writer).[8]

Reformation writer Marie Dentière writes of equality in Christ:

I ask, did not Jesus die as much for the poor ignorant people and the idiots as for my dear sirs the shaved, tonsured, and mitred? Did he preach and spread my Gospel so much only for my dear sirs the wise and important doctors? Isn't it for all of us? Do we have two Gospels, one for men and another for women? One for the wise and another for the fools? Are we not one in our Lord?[9]

As I near the close of this chapter, I think of one of my teachers, Christian ethicist Stanley Hauerwas. Hauerwas taught me that I can't abandon the church even though church is so very hard, and he taught me that I can never be casual about church unity. He is rather more romantic about Roman Catholic life than I think reality supports, but he is also quite right that

[8]Karen E. Spierling, "Women, Marriage, and Family," in *T&T Clark Companion to Reformation Theology*, ed. David M. Whitford (London: Bloomsbury, 2012), 187.
[9]Quoted in Spierling, "Women, Marriage, and Family," 188, from "Epistle to Marguerite de Navarre and Preface to a Sermon by John Calvin," ed. and trans. Mary B. McKinley, in *The Other Voice in Early Modern Europe* (Chicago: University of Chicago Press, 2004).

Roman Catholicism sustains unity together with diversity in way Protestants have not always been good at doing:

> As I oftentimes point out, it is extraordinary that Catholicism is able to keep the Irish and the Italians in the same church. What an achievement! Perhaps equally amazing is their ability to keep within the same church Jesuits, Dominicans, and Franciscans. I think Catholics are able to do that because they know that their unity does not depend upon everyone agreeing. Indeed, they can celebrate their disagreements because they understand that our unity is founded upon the cross and resurrection of Jesus of Nazareth that makes the Eucharist possible. They do not presume, therefore, that unity requires that we all read Scripture the same way.[10]

Here Hauerwas coheres with Phillip Cary's suggestion that the unity of the community of Scripture brings us to Jesus and not to propositional unanimity.

I love doctrine. I do not envision a church without such, but knowing Jesus is knowing a person, not reciting a list of claims, and the ability to claim the "right" propositions is nothing without union with Christ, which transforms us in love. That I'm not Roman Catholic or Eastern Orthodox is not finally about some conviction that those traditions are fundamentally, propositionally wrong. Given that I've critiqued Roman Catholic and Eastern Orthodox doctrinal commitments in this book, arguing instead for classic Protestant doctrinal claims, this might seem odd. The thing is, I love propositions. I find a

---

[10]Stanley Hauerwas, *Sanctify Them in the Truth: Holiness Exemplified* (Nashville: Abingdon, 1999), 256-57.

wellspring of nerdy joy in digging into conversations about reading Scripture well and how we come to affirm certain propositions. I love the story of doctrine as it lives across centuries and cultures, and I love to imagine how some doctrinal truth might take shape in the time and space to which I'm called. I find many typically Protestant propositions quite convincing, and some of them I want to reclaim in a slightly contrarian way (deny the perspicuity of Scripture? What fun is that?). But Hauerwas is right; "our unity is founded upon the cross and resurrection of Jesus of Nazareth that makes the Eucharist possible." We're one in Christ Jesus.

SEVEN

HOPES FOR CHRISTIAN
UNITY IN DIVERSITY

I PRAY THAT THE PRACTICE of Protestant Christian faith is done in the hope of Christian unity. I believe that Christian unity need not shut down Christian diversity. This world tends to say otherwise, as though unity and diversity were threats to each other and we must choose the "right" side at the expense of the other. But I must believe that the church, when viewed in the kingdom's light, is not a playing field with sides, where some must lose for others to win. The church is not a playing field at all, though it may be a city with plenty of parks and gardens. The church is a circle centered on the throne of the Lamb, and the traditions of the church may be gathered in from every direction, each tradition still itself, each needing to discard what is it has clung to that proves contrary to the gospel, and each and all drawing just as near to the Lamb. The church has room for all to worship, bringing the beloved particularities of our diversity into unity around that throne. This must be true, if the Lamb on the throne is the Prince of Peace, a slaughtered lamb and not a conquering warlord, for the church must share the character of the One on that throne.

ONE FONT, ONE TABLE

When my children were small, we had a lovely picture book called *Bread, Bread, Bread*.[1] It's a simple book of photos of children and families from many parts of the world. All are eating bread. There are many different kinds—bagels, baguettes, naan, and so on—but all the bread is bread, and it feeds all the people. Reading this book to a child opens a delightful window into cognitive development, as the book calls the reader to see that all the different breads can be one thing. Below the level of the text, the book makes a similar call on the reader to recognize the unity of diverse humanity.

It is fitting that the waters of baptism and the bread of heaven should be the central signs of the church. Like the church itself, these signs are universal mysteries, and these signs unite us even when they must do so in spite of us. We often speak of baptism and the Supper as areas of division and difference in the body. Whether we know details or not, many Protestants are aware that something about practicing the sacraments played a role in the divisions of the Reformation, and it is true that differences in sacramental theology continue to divide us, but there is also another story here. I think this story goes to the heart of the graced character of the church, and it is ours in the truth of that grace, however we might try to disrupt it. The story of sacraments is not only one of discord. I'm going to make a small effort here to tell it as a story of unity.

---

[1] Ann Morris, *Bread, Bread, Bread (Food of the World)*, photographs by Ken Heyman (repr., San Francisco: HarperCollins, 1993).

Let's start with a standard definition of a sacrament: a visible sign of a spiritual grace. Sacraments, by their very nature, are places of unity. They are places where the spiritual and material worlds come together, and that coming together is a grace for a specific kind of creature: the human, who is both spiritual and material. In sacrament, the material signs matter. That is, it is not random that water is the sign of baptism, bread and cup the sign of the Supper. It would not do just as well to use mud for baptism or caviar for the Supper. The signs matter. They have material and spiritual meaning. Water means something different than does mud, and the meaning of water is attached and integral to the grace of baptism just as the meaning of bread is attached to the grace of the Supper. More, these meanings or resonances are (relatively) universal. All diverse humans, all the time and everywhere, feel the meaning of water as it quenches thirst, washes, and comes forth with birth, and those meanings are tied together with the grace of baptism. All people of the Scriptures share the water; the United Methodist baptismal liturgy gathers up these meanings beautifully while organizing them into a triune structure, which culminates in calling on the Spirit's power to work in this sign. Calling on the Father, the liturgy names God sweeping "across the dark waters" and God's work in saving "those on the ark through water," as well as God's work in leading the people "to freedom through the sea." Turning to Jesus, the liturgy connects his incarnation in Mary's womb with baptism:

> In the fullness of time you sent Jesus,
> nurtured in the water of a womb.
> He was baptized by John and anointed by your Spirit.
> He called his disciples

to share in the baptism of his death and resurrection
and to make disciples of all nations.

Finally, the liturgy calls on the Spirit to "bless this gift of water and those who receive it, to wash away their sin."[2] As with water, so with bread and cup. These signs are of daily, ordinary nourishment. They are of feeding and growth. They are signs that matter. The very basic, shared, human meaning of these signs comes with a kind of unity that no church rebellion can break as long as we continue to share in those signs. However we disagree, water will be water, signifying new birth; bread will be bread, satisfying our hunger. There's a givenness to the signs themselves that prevents us from erasing the unity they create.[3]

While we may know that sacramental theology was part of the rifts of the Reformation, we may not focus on the sacramental unity that did and does remain. While Luther objected to many features of late medieval Roman Catholic sacramental theology, it's important to remember that there is much he did not and would not reject. He remained convinced of the centrality of the sacraments. He remained certain that God's grace comes to us in and with these material signs. Baptisms are baptisms because the church is grace and not works. Many divided Christians continue to practice a vague, and perhaps uneasy, ecumenicity here, accepting (often) baptisms from churches

---

2"The Baptismal Covenant I," in *Book of Worship* (Nashville: United Methodist Publishing House, 2009), www.umcdiscipleship.org/book-of-worship/the-baptismal-covenant-i.
3Peter Leithart, a Protestant who holds what I've called an "institutional account" of church unity, disagrees. Leithart says, "We celebrate the same sacraments of baptism and the Lord's Supper. To that degree we are united. But it is a low degree of union" (Peter Leithart, *The End of Protestantism: Pursuing Unity in a Fragmented Church* [Grand Rapids, MI: Brazos, 2016], 3). Leithart's claim seems to me instead to entail an unintentionally low view of the sacraments, attaching far too much importance to human understanding and practice and not enough import to God's mighty work therein. What could be a higher degree of union than that worked by divine grace in baptism and the Supper?

from which they are divided. The unity of baptism is an ontological reality, whether we know it or like it or not. But we are called to learn to know it and like it. We're called to "walk in a manner worthy" of the calling that is ours in the unbreakable oneness of the one God of all:

> I, therefore, the prisoner in the Lord, beg you to walk in a manner worthy of the calling to which you have been called, with all humility and gentleness, with patience, bearing with one another in love, making every effort to maintain the unity of the Spirit in the bond of peace: there is one body and one Spirit, just as you were called to the one hope of your calling, one Lord, one faith, one baptism, one God and Father of all, who is above all and through all and in all. (Eph 4:1-6)

Paul treats our one baptism as a given from which we can and must proceed. He calls us to remember "that all of us who were baptized into Christ Jesus were baptized into his death" (Rom 6:3). More, we're called to remember that we have been united with Jesus in that baptism. If Jesus is the basis of our unity, how can we be truly divided? If Jesus is the basis of our unity, we are being called to "live with him" (Rom 6:8) in a life that reflects that unity. Even though we persist in dividing our tables, those tables persist in uniting us with the one Lord Jesus Christ. I find tremendous hope in the one who presides at one table, shared by Eastern Orthodox, Roman Catholic, Protestant, and all Christians.

A GLOBAL FAITH

The people swimming in this one font and eating at this one table are a diverse people. They represent many countries, nations, tribes, ethnic groups, and cultures. They hail from many centuries and continents. Their many bodies—encompassing diversities of class, gender, race, background, beauty, and story—form one body, with Christ as head. Rightly honoring the unity of the church requires recognizing, dignifying, and celebrating this diversity. The church is even bigger than the usual Western designations of Protestant, Roman Catholic, and Eastern Orthodox allow. There are diversities within each of those traditions and outside those traditions. Some Anabaptists do not understand themselves to be Protestant. I'm not convinced by that argument, but it represents something about the diversity within Protestantism, including the deep discomfort some traditions have with what they see as Protestant Christianity's inherent collusion with state power. (Again, I'm not convinced, but I am only interested in participating in a version of Protestantism that rejects such a collusion.) The non-Chalcedonian churches, including the Ethiopian, Coptic, Armenian, Syrian, Indian, and Eritrean Churches, represent an ancient branch of Christianity with a narrative that does not fit that which divides the church into Eastern Orthodox, Roman Catholic, and Protestant branches.[4]

New contextual and local branches of church continue to emerge in great strength around the world, from the Independent African Churches to charismatic groups in Latin America, and these new churches bear a variety of relationships, all including some measure of continuity and discontinuity, to the old Roman Catholic and Protestant missionary churches.[5]

---

[4]See Augustine Casiday, *The Orthodox Christian World* (London: Routledge, 2012).

[5]Philip Jenkins, *The Next Christendom: The Coming of Global Christianity*, 3rd ed. (Oxford: Oxford University Press, 2011).

While I think it's right to identify much of this new church growth as "Protestant," it would look mightily strange to a seventeenth-century Presbyterian in Scotland or a twenty-first-century Lutheran in Wisconsin. Philip Jenkins summarizes some of the new character of global church growth:

> The types of Christianity that have thrived most success-fully in the global South have been very different from what many Europeans and North Americans consider mainstream. These models have been far more enthusi-astic, much more centrally concerned with the immediate workings of the supernatural, through prophecy, visions, ecstatic utterances, and healing. . . . When we look at the Pentecostal enthusiasm of present-day Brazil, or the indig-enous churches of Africa, then quite possibly we are getting a foretaste of the Christianity of the next generation.[6]

The church is big and weird and wild and wonderful. It is dif-ficult to categorize and often resists being slotted into boxes created by sociologists, historians, or theologians. This is part of the very nature and beauty of the church.

If the one church of Jesus Christ is one, it is also holy, catholic, and apostolic. For theologian Lamin Sanneh, the Christian church must be flexible by its very nature, or it cannot be the global church. Sanneh emphasizes the nature of Christian Scripture as translatable, able to be the authentic Word of God in any culture, context, and language. Church unity can only be a unity of diversity and flexibility or it will be a false unity, which proclaims itself whole while cutting off any number of parts of the body. Again, says Sanneh, "we do not threaten one another

---

[6]Jenkins, *Next Christendom*, 122.

by coming into God's presence with the variety of tongue and race that marks our humanity."[7]

DIVERSITY HONORS GOD'S LOVE OF CONTEXT

In the story in Genesis, we are invited to imagine a world undivided linguistically, a "whole earth" of "one language and the same words" (Gen 11:1). Then, humans go and try to solidify this unity into power. They want to "make a name" for themselves lest they be "scattered abroad" (Gen 11:4). It is interesting here that the people building that doomed tower are afraid of losing the simple unity they possess. The Lord brings down the people and their tower, confusing language "so that they will not understand one another's speech" (Gen 11:7), and what happens is precisely what the people feared; "from there the LORD scattered them abroad over the face of all the earth" (Gen 11:9). Why do the tower builders fear the scattering? And how does God redeem Babel?

The specific and surprising way God heals the division of Babel can be emblematic for how we understand diversity in the church. We find that healing in the Pentecost account in the book of Acts. We might have expected God to erase the division between the people of many nations by giving them one tongue: an official language for the people of God. Instead, God honors the many tongues and particularities gathered there: "All of them were filled with the Holy Spirit and began to speak in other languages, as the Spirit gave them ability" (Acts 2:4). I want to quote the passage at length to honor the many nations named, as the Spirit did that day:

---

[7]Lamin Sanneh, *Whose Religion Is Christianity: The Gospel Beyond the West* (Grand Rapids, MI: Eerdmans, 2003), 107.

And at this sound the crowd gathered and was bewildered, because each one heard them speaking in the native language of each. Amazed and astonished, they asked, "Are not all these who are speaking Galileans? And how is it that we hear, each of us, in our own native language? Parthians, Medes, Elamites, and residents of Mesopotamia, Judea and Cappadocia, Pontus and Asia, Phrygia and Pamphylia, Egypt and the parts of Libya belonging to Cyrene, and visitors from Rome, both Jews and proselytes, Cretans and Arabs—in our own languages we hear them speaking about God's deeds of power." (Acts 2:6-11)

This honoring of diversity is met with mixed reactions. Some are amazed. Others assume that the whole crowd must be drunk.

But this is the surprising way the Spirit works. The Spirit does not bring unity by erasing difference. The Spirit brings unity by enabling understanding across difference. Per Kevin Vanhoozer:

Various Protestant streams testify to Jesus in their own vocabularies, and it takes many languages (i.e. interpretive traditions) to minister the meaning of God's Word and the fullness of Christ. As the body is made up of many members, so many interpretations may be needed to do justice to the body of the biblical text. Why else are there four Gospels, but that the one story of Jesus was too rich to be told from one perspective only? Could it be that the various Protestant traditions function similarly as witnesses who testify to the same Jesus from different situations and perspectives?[8]

---

[8]Kevin J. Vanhoozer, *Biblical Authority After Babel: Retrieving the Solas in the Spirit of Mere Protestant Christianity* (Grand Rapids, MI: Brazos, 2018), 223.

Maybe the final healing of the church—in which we are so visibly one that the world can't help but see—will not be a healing in which all the dissidents come home to the true church, whether imagined as Roman Catholic or Eastern Orthodox or fundamentalist Baptist. Maybe it will be a healing in which we all persist, truly hearing each other, truly seeing each other, gathered in unity around the throne of the Lamb.

EIGHT

SCRIPTURE PASSAGES FOR PROTESTANTS

IN A BOOK IN WHICH I've argued for the strength of the Protestant principle *sola scriptura*, it seems appropriate to spend some time dwelling with a few passages of Scripture, both in fidelity to that principle and as examples of my own thinking about how that principle works in Protestant life. Every passage of Scripture ought to interest Protestants, for Protestant theology confesses "plenary inspiration," the belief that the Spirit's inspiring work extends through the whole of the Scriptures. We aren't meant to pick and choose those bits we like best. We're meant to live with the whole thing as God's revelatory word to us and for us.

This makes my task in this chapter complicated. How does one choose a few biblical passages for Protestants? One temptation is to select my favorites, texts that have spoken to me of the love of God and warmed my heart.[1] I'd question the truth of any claim to avoid this route entirely, and I don't believe such avoidance is even the best option. Liking a passage may well

---

[1] If you checked this footnote for a John Wesley reference, thank you.

help an author to communicate well about said passage. I've gone ahead and chosen one personal favorite, from Ephesians 2. Another temptation is to select those passages that seem most obviously and screamingly Protestant, and here again, I've chosen one passage that might fit the bill, those famous scriptural words about the nature of Scripture from 2 Timothy. For what it's worth, this passage is not a favorite for me, or, rather, it's taken time and the work of the Spirit for it to grow on me.

A third route through choosing texts for this chapter could have been found in selecting passages where there is a clear and obvious difference in Protestant interpretation compared to Roman Catholic and Eastern Orthodox readings. The most obvious passage here might be Peter's encounter with Jesus (see Mt 16:13-20) in which he recognizes Jesus as "Messiah, the Son of the living God," and Jesus returns that this is the rock on which his church will be built. (Here Roman Catholics tend to identify the rock as Peter himself, the first pope, while Protestants see the rock as Peter's confession of Jesus' identity.) In the interest of unity in diversity, I've opted to forgo this third route, choosing instead a passage Protestants may be tempted to neglect but in which I hope all Christians can find shared vision, Mary's song, in which she magnifies the Lord.

As the concluding chapter in this book, I've shaped this chapter to reflect something of my hopes for Protestant theology, Protestant embrace of the authority of Scripture, and Protestant biblical interpretation, without which that embrace will fail. In this chapter, I'm trying to follow the storyteller's maxim "show, don't tell," trying to bear witness to my theology in the act of hermeneutics rather than telling how I might do so.

My attempt here is radically imperfect, but I submit it in the hope that it might draw you back to these words, to the Word, in ways that will help the one church in our task of witnessing to grace for the broken and healing for all who would turn to Jesus.

PUTTING TO DEATH THAT HOSTILITY, EPHESIANS 2:11-22

So then, remember that at one time you Gentiles by birth, called "the uncircumcision" by those who are called "the circumcision"—a circumcision made in the flesh by human hands—remember that you were at that time without Christ, being aliens from the commonwealth of Israel and strangers to the covenants of promise, having no hope and without God in the world. But now in Christ Jesus you who once were far off have been brought near by the blood of Christ. For he is our peace; in his flesh he has made both into one and has broken down the dividing wall, that is, the hostility between us, abolishing the law with its commandments and ordinances, that he might create in himself one new humanity in place of the two, thus making peace, and might reconcile both to God in one body through the cross, thus putting to death that hostility through it. So he came and proclaimed peace to you who were far off and peace to those who were near, for through him both of us have access in one Spirit to the Father. So then, you are no longer strangers and aliens, but you are fellow citizens with the saints and also members of the household of God, built upon the foundation of the apostles and prophets, with Christ Jesus himself as the cornerstone; in him the whole structure is joined together and grows into a holy temple in the Lord, in whom you also are built together spiritually into a dwelling place for God.

In his *Confessions*, Augustine recounts his long search for truth and his transformation in Christ. Key to that account is an event in which he learns to interpret Scripture together with another, the bishop and teacher Ambrose of Milan. Augustine had hoped that the Manichean teacher Faustus would answer his many questions about Scripture, but when he met Faustus, he was deeply unimpressed. This discouraging encounter started to "loosen the snare" of Manicheanism for Augustine. Then Augustine moved to Milan, where he encountered Ambrose. In conversation with this new teacher and friend, Augustine was persuaded that Christian belief was reasonable, and many of his previous misconceptions about Christianity were corrected. All of this is to say that the account of biblical interpretation in *Confessions* is deeply social. Ambrose took Augustine "up as a father takes a newborn baby in his arms." Ambrose's ability to interpret Scripture in ways Augustine found intellectually persuasive paved the way for Augustine's allegiance to Christ. Augustine tells us, "I fell in love with him, as it were, not at first as a teacher of the truth . . . but simply as a person who was kind to me."[2] The language of desire plays here, just as it does throughout the work.

Augustine's attraction to Ambrose was not sexual, but desire *is* the right category for it. Theologian Sarah Coakley writes

---

[2] Augustine, *Confessions*, trans. Maria Boulding (New York: Vintage, 1998), 5.13, 5.23.

about the church's deep need for what she calls "erotic saints."[3] She's not talking about sex any more than is Augustine when he falls in love with Ambrose; she's talking about people who are so attractive in their persons, their stories, and their embodied lives that others are drawn to them and want to be like them in their own embodied lives. She sees our culture of celebrity and images as one in which we're constantly attracted to people who are the very opposite of saints, and she worries that the body of Christ is failing to be the kind of attractive body that compels as a real alternative to this false desire.

What does this have to do with Ephesians 2? There's a sense in which Augustine's hermeneutical journey mirrors my own, particularly regarding this epistle. Frankly, I wasn't fond of Ephesians. I don't know that I had read it very carefully, but I had reduced the book to submission, "wives to your husbands," and when I took my first academic class on the New Testament, the instructor treated Ephesians as a problem to be solved by explaining away Pauline authorship. This sat oddly with me, but I didn't have the tools to do much more with it. A decade later, I'd had better hermeneutical tools in hand for some time, but I had never really revisited Ephesians until a small group I was part of decided to read it together. (In some ways, what could be more paradigmatically Protestant than that small group Bible study?!) My eyes and heart were opened. This was a deliciously nerdy group; we bought a copy of Klyne Snodgrass's excellent commentary and passed it around each week.[4] We also included a couple of literature scholars and poets, a chemist

---

[3]Sarah Coakley, *The New Asceticism: Sexuality, Gender and the Quest for God* (London: Bloomsbury, 2016).

[4]Klyne Snodgrass, *Ephesians*, NIV Application Commentary 10 (Grand Rapids, MI: Zondervan, 2009).

and a physicist, and a few pastors, and the insights brought to the text from these areas of expertise were beautiful, but what really changed my reading of Ephesians was not a set of (fantastic) intellectual observations. What changed came in reading with a group of beautiful, holy, fascinating, faithful friends and inviting the Spirit to work in our conversations about the text and in our lives. Like Augustine with Ambrose, I too "fell in love," and I learned from and with these saints what it could mean for a text to live and act in human lives.

I learned to read Ephesians as a gospel story. I learned to live in that story. I remembered that I was one who had been "without Christ," alien "from the commonwealth of Israel," a stranger to the "covenants of promise" (Eph 2:12). As I felt this, praying in the company of poets and scientists and saints, I was able to connect hermeneutical tools I'd been acquiring for years to a text I had never really thought about as speaking to me. I thought about how theologian Willie Jennings taught me that I'm a Gentile, how he opened my eyes to the error of the (White, American) Christian who assumes she is the near one, the child of the promise, and forgets she is the outsider who has been grafted in by grace.[5] I remembered how he'd helped me to see the heresy of racism through this lens, and while I'd thought I'd absorbed Jennings's argument years before, it was now, in this company of saints, that his lessons became part of my body and not just my intellect. Then, before I could turn that realization to useless self-flagellation, I was struck by the Word announcing peace *both* "to you who were far off and peace to those who were near, for through him both of us have access in one Spirit

---

[5]Willie Jennings, *The Christian Imagination: Theology and the Origins of Race* (New Haven, CT: Yale University Press, 2011).

to the Father" (Eph 2:17-18), and the Spirit moved to break down dividing walls in my heart, body, mind, relationships, church life. . . .

As a theology nerd, I love this passage in Ephesians for being laden with doctrine. In it, I find church and spirit, Christology, soteriology, ministry, ecclesiology, epistemology, hermeneutics, politics, sociology, and more, but all those things are bare without the life-giving power of the Spirit known in embracing the Word in community. When that power is there, though, those things become more vital. Here I could well be accused of being rather a mess hermeneutically; I've invoked theologians from the fourth and the twenty-first centuries and, with them, social contexts that aren't that of the first-century human author of the text, though I've also mentioned a biblical studies commentary. I've involved feelings and the intellect; both may be objectionable to some, and neither lends itself to a neat and tidy interpretative system. One might worry, in fact, that I'm being downright sub-Protestant, dragging the church and my personal friends into the work of biblical interpretation. I'll leave it to my argument earlier in this book to explain why I think I'm being vitally Protestant. *Sola scriptura* is not Scripture isolated behind locked doors; the authority of Scripture is authoritative in the world, in the church, in conversation with the mess. The authority of Scripture lives most happily in this kind of surprising and life-giving hermeneutical carnival.

ABLE TO INSTRUCT YOU FOR SALVATION, 2 TIMOTHY 3:10-17

Now you have observed my teaching, my conduct, my aim in life, my faith, my patience, my love, my steadfastness, my persecutions, and my sufferings, the things that happened to me in Antioch, Iconium, and Lystra. What persecutions I endured! Yet the Lord rescued me from all of them. Indeed, all who want to live a godly life in Christ Jesus will be persecuted. But wicked people and impostors will go from bad to worse, deceiving others and being deceived. But as for you, continue in what you have learned and firmly believed, knowing from whom you learned it and how from childhood you have known sacred writings that are able to instruct you for salvation through faith in Christ Jesus. All scripture is inspired by God and is useful for teaching, for reproof, for correction, and for training in righteousness, so that the person of God may be proficient, equipped for every good work.

Here is the one text of Scripture about Scripture Protestant Christians are most likely to have memorized. That is, many of us have memorized 2 Timothy 3:16, learning "all scripture is inspired by God and is useful for. . . ." I have no inherent complaint about this practice. This is a great biblical locus for summarizing the claims Scripture makes about its own nature and authority, and while that idea is sometimes dismissed with a reminder that Timothy would have been thinking of Israel's Scriptures and not of the writings Christians call the New Testament, I'm unimpressed with that dismissal. As the New Testament is Christian Scripture, it makes perfect sense to include it, by extension, in the description of Scripture here. Second Timothy 3:16 is a fine "memory verse," and it's both unsurprising and appropriate that Protestant catechesis should turn us to it, for it distills much of the Protestant principle of *sola scriptura*.

Yet, wherever we find a single verse of Scripture used popularly and frequently by itself, we'll have much to learn by returning to the context of that verse and weighing it considering the verses immediately around it, the book in which it is found, and the canon as a whole. This claim also fits with the best of Protestant understanding of the authority of Scripture. Here we find, again, that the authority of Scripture operates relationally. This claim does not negate the existence here of propositional truth in and about the Scriptures. That is, among other things, those Scriptures are "inspired" and "useful." But how is Timothy meant to know this in his bones? The textual answer rests in part in his relationship with Paul, who reminds Timothy that he has "observed" a great many things in Paul's person, including "teaching," "conduct," and "aim in life," as well as, Paul says, "my faith, my patience, my love, my steadfastness," and, finally, soberingly, but perhaps also most persuasively, "my persecutions, and my sufferings."

Paul, a man of the Scriptures, is a certain kind of man. He teaches and believes certain propositional truths, but he also lives his life in a way that reflects the truth of the God of the Scriptures. Timothy's knowledge of Paul is knowledge of his love. That love is one that is likely to lead Timothy, like Paul, into suffering and persecution, and Timothy will need that love to endure. Paul seems confident of that endurance, for Timothy should "continue in what you have learned and firmly believed, knowing from whom you learned it." That last bit—"knowing from whom you have learned it"—is key to the operation of biblical truth and authority. The "whom" includes Paul here, but it also includes Timothy's grandma and mama, for Timothy's faith "lived first" in them (2 Tim 1:5). It turns out that Lois (grandmother) and Eunice (mother) are key to the authority of

Scripture, for Timothy and for us, as we continue to learn the faith that lived in them. Know from whom you have learned it: Paul, Lois, Eunice, the many saints of God, perhaps your grandma, like Timothy's, or your Sunday school teacher, or your friend, in whom you knew love, and—most importantly—from Jesus Christ himself, whose authority is his person. We receive that authority in personal relationship with him.

The biblical faith of Paul, Timothy, Lois, and Eunice is a living and active faith. Again, the authority of Scripture goes beyond the propositional ("I believe that Scripture is the inspired Word of God") into the embodied. Scripture changes us: our neurons, our habits, our schedules, and our relationships. Scripture works. Scripture works in human lives. Scripture does things; it teaches. It reproves, corrects, and trains us in righteousness. Scripture shapes us into certain kinds of people; it molds people in whose conduct, aim in life, love, and steadfastness others may glimpse Jesus. It builds up a people who will be ready to endure suffering for the sake of the love of Jesus Christ, in whose faith we are being saved and equipped for "every good work" (2 Tim 3:17). Scripture works good works, and good works are key to the authority of Scripture. We are equipped for them because we know Jesus: "I know the one in whom I have put my trust, and I am sure that he is able to guard until that day the deposit I have entrusted to him" (2 Tim 1:12).

THE MIGHTY ONE HAS DONE GREAT THINGS, LUKE 1:46-55

And Mary said,

"My soul magnifies the Lord,
    and my spirit rejoices in God my Savior,

for he has looked with favor on the lowly state of
    his servant.
  Surely from now on all generations will call
    me blessed,
for the Mighty One has done great things for me,
    and holy is his name;
indeed, his mercy is for those who fear him
    from generation to generation.
He has shown strength with his arm;
    he has scattered the proud in the imagination of
      their hearts.
He has brought down the powerful from their thrones
    and lifted up the lowly;
he has filled the hungry with good things
    and sent the rich away empty.
He has come to the aid of his child Israel,
    in remembrance of his mercy,
according to the promise he made to our ancestors,
    to Abraham and to his descendants forever."

As the last of our Scripture passages for Protestants, I've chosen Mary's song as a passage in which Christians of all traditions should find strength and sustenance, but it's also a passage Protestants may give too little attention because Protestants sometimes get squeamish about too much talk about Mary, afraid that such talk is somehow less than Protestant or prone to lead to specific Roman Catholic teachings about Mary that Protestants generally find extrabiblical and problematic.[6] We Protestants need not fear Mary. We certainly ought not ignore

---

[6]That is, teachings about Mary as sinless, her perpetual virginity, and her assumption into heaven, along with Roman Catholic doctrine about the papal office, which undergirds some

her. Here she is, in Scripture itself. Here she is, a model of faith. Here she is, interpreting Scripture, appropriating Scripture to her own life, glorifying the God who has done great things.

Mary's response to God's work in her life is of great importance. God sends the angel Gabriel: "Greetings, favored one! The Lord is with you" (Lk 1:28). The angel announces that Mary will conceive Jesus, but this announcement is not a command. It is an invitation. Responding in faith, Mary places herself in accord with God's invitation: "Here am I, the servant of the Lord; let it be with me according to your word" (Lk 1:38). In this, Mary is a paradigm of God's work in human lives; she is a sign of faith. For centuries, interpreters of Scripture have drawn our attention to Mary's vital yes to God's desire to work in her life.[7] Contemporary New Testament scholars Beverly Gaventa and Scot McKnight read Luke with this tradition. Gaventa sees a double meaning in "Mary's response"; that response both is Mary's "consent to the role of the Mother of Jesus" and "identifies another central theme, that of the consent of human beings to God's will."[8] Mary is paradigmatic of all human beings. McKnight emphasizes the dangerousness of Mary's pregnancy and so helps us see how "Mary's 'may it be' was an act of courageous faith."[9] Gaventa elaborates parallels

---

of these teachings as dogmatic because they were proclaimed under the pope's authority. Mary's song is also called "the Magnificat," from the first word in the Latin translation.

[7] Thomas Aquinas, *Summa Theologica* III, question 30, answer 1; Martin Luther, *Martin Luther's Christmas Book*, ed. Roland H. Bainton (Minneapolis: Augsburg, 1948), 14-16; Irenaeus, *Against Heresies* 3.22.4 (this is a contrast between Mary's obedience in the annunciation and Eve's disobedience); Luigi Gambero, *Mary and the Fathers of the Church: The Blessed Virgin Mary in Patristic Thought*, trans. Thomas Buffer (San Francisco: Ignatius Press, 1991).

[8] Beverly Roberts Gaventa, "'Nothing Will Be Impossible with God': Mary as the Mother of Believers," in *Mary, Mother of God*, ed. Carl E. Braaten and Robert W. Jenson (Grand Rapids, MI: Eerdmans, 2004), 19.

[9] Scot McKnight, *The Real Mary: Why Evangelical Christians Can Embrace the Mother of Jesus* (Brewster, MA: Paraclete, 2007), 9.

between Mary's story and the earlier story of Sarah learning of the coming birth of Isaac. Mary's faith is the antithesis of Sarah's laughter, and that faith will be interpreted in Mary's life through both word and deed. Mary's faith pours forth in song, and that song confirms this reading of the key nature of Mary's consent and helps us see what it means to live by faith. The God of the Magnificat is the God who lifts up the lowly, the God who works by mercy and relationship. The Spirit envelops Mary, so that with the Spirit she can do the work of magnifying and rejoicing as God lifts her up.

When "we receive Mary's story as our own," we are brought into the dynamics of mystery that are always there when we try to understand how God works in human lives.[10] Mary's faith is not, to use the word in the old Protestant sense, a "work" she performs. Her consent is as all human consent must be; it requires divine power to for its possibility. Gaventa elaborates:

> The difference between receiving Mary's story and imitating Mary needs to be clarified. . . . What is it of Mary that we take in, provided that the Lukan story has its way with us? It is, of course, Mary's consent to God's intervention in her life, her exultation in God's redemption, her pondering the meaning of Jesus, and certainly her persevering presence with other believers. We take in her confidence that truly all things are possible with God. This way of putting things coheres with Luke's larger story, precisely because Luke does not show us human beings setting out to find God—to be better and better disciples—but God reaching for human beings. By identifying Mary as our

---

[10]Gaventa, "Nothing Will Be Impossible," 34.

Mother, we do not so much elevate Mary as recognize in her story the fundamental Lukan claim that nothing will be impossible with God, not even our consent to God's will.[11]

Or, in the words of Serene Jones, the "story of Mary illustrates what happens when we understand [the doctrine of total depravity] not as disparaging human beings but as recognizing the condition they find themselves in. . . . The impossible things God does are done for us and with us, creatively replacing those paradigms that we have presumed are the only possibilities."[12]

In Mary, Luther sees a revelation of salvation by grace alone, faith alone, Christ alone. Luther invites us, in this faith, to become one with the incarnate Jesus, to "make his birth your own . . . rid yourself of your birth and receive, instead, his." He continues, "By this token, you sit assuredly in the Virgin Mary's lap and are her dear child."[13]

---

[11]Gaventa, "Nothing Will Be Impossible," 34-35.

[12]Serene Jones, *Trauma and Grace: Theology in a Ruptured World* (Louisville, KY: Westminster John Knox Press, 2009), 117.

[13]Martin Luther, "The Gospel for Christmas Eve Luke 2:1-14," in *Luther's Works*, American ed. (Philadelphia: Fortress, 1974), 52:16.

EPILOGUE

HARRISON SCOTT KEY weaves the story of his marriage together with the stories of several different churches. He contrasts the beautiful and stately tradition of the big, respectable downtown church he once attended with the broken mess of the church in which he and his family finally find a home for their own deep brokenness. They must leave behind the church of the façade, one of too many churches that turn out to be "Disney parks of make-believe." Key says, "Despite its glorious architecture and many beautiful traditions and the good people who tried to be my friend, this place was not a safe place for my family. We didn't need beatific and pious masquerades. We needed the masks ripped right off." They find a broken church in a broken building, a struggling little place populated by people from diverse Christian traditions, a place "that didn't hide brokenness, because brokenness was everywhere, including many of the lights."[1] He continues:

---

[1]Harrison Scott Key, *How to Stay Married: The Most Insane Love Story Ever Told* (New York: Avid Reader, 2023), 110, 111, 142.

Love lived in the people of our new church, others, like us, in exile, refugees from abuse and scandal and estrangement, people who were far from home or from right up the street. The only thing that needed to be excommunicated from my home was the idol of perfect obedience: hers or mine. Our story was no fairy tale. A church with broken windows is just what we needed: the community that would make us whole again and pull us through what had happened, and what was yet to come.[2]

That, my friends, is why I'm Protestant. This is no fairy land. This is hard. Not only can I not pretend the windows aren't broken, but I need them to be broken. It is in brokenness that we find healing. The one loaf can only feed us all when it has been broken and broken and broken again:

> But we have this treasure in clay jars, so that it may be made clear that this extraordinary power belongs to God and does not come from us. We are afflicted in every way but not crushed, perplexed but not driven to despair, persecuted but not forsaken, struck down but not destroyed. . . . So we do not lose heart. Even though our outer nature is wasting away, our inner nature is being renewed day by day. For our slight, momentary affliction is producing for us an eternal weight of glory beyond all measure, because we look not at what can be seen but at what cannot be seen, for what can be seen is temporary, but what cannot be seen is eternal. (2 Cor 4:7-9, 16-18)

The Japanese art of *kintsugi* has become a focal image of the church for me. The *kintsugi* master uses pieces of a broken

---

[2]Key, *How to Stay Married*, 145.

object and mends them, using gold lacquer. From an interview with artist Makoto Fujimura by Chris Carter:

> The restored pieces are so coveted that they often sell at a price higher than before. But for a mended vessel to attain this value, the *kintsugi* master spends extended periods getting to know the cup's fragments. Only after he was intimately familiar with the jagged edges would he apply adhesive. Though the process was long, it results in a vessel whose cracks weren't hidden but accentuated in gold. "*Kintsugi*," Mako reflects, "is taking broken ceramics and saying, 'That's not the end; it's only the beginning.'" The shattered vessel, in the hands of a skilled *kintsugi* master, becomes a new creation rendered more beautiful because of its brokenness.[3]

All my pessimism about the church, all my conviction that the whole thing is a broken mess, is not pessimism at the end of the day.[4] In the already/not-yet light of resurrection, it's an affirmation of the beauty of God and of what God is doing in the one, beautiful, honest, broken and healing church of Jesus Christ.

---

[3]Makoto Fujimura, interviewed by Chris Carter, "Mended to Make," Ekstasis, 2023, www.ekstasismagazine.com/visual-artists/2023/makoto-fujimura.

[4]I'm a Wesleyan, after all.

GENERAL INDEX

Anabaptist tradition, 120

Anglican, 55, 62, 103

Apostles' Creed, 23

Aquinas, Thomas, 9, 136

Arianism, 12-13

Augustine, 9, 27-28, 34, 39, 45-53, 103, 128-30

authority of Scripture, 42, 44, 56, 84, 126, 131, 133-34

    see also *sola scriptura*

baptism, 27, 50-51, 56-58, 77, 109, 116-19

    see also sacraments

Boleyn, Anne, 63-64

Cary, Phillip, 89-91, 97

Catherine of Aragon, 63-64

catholic church, 23, 25-27, 36, 47, 49, 51

catholicity, 23-25, 27, 28, 35

Chalcedon

    see councils

Church of England, 62

Constantine, 47

councils

    of Chalcedon, 10-11, 13-14, 32

    early ecumenical, 10-11

    of Nicaea, 10-11, 12, 32

Diocletian, 47-48

Donatism, 27-28, 39

    controversy, 47-52

Eastern Orthodox tradition, 6, 10, 14, 21-22, 26, 28, 30, 44-47, 53, 56, 61-62, 70, 76, 81, 101, 109, 113, 120, 126

ecclesiology, 38, 44-55, 59-68, 70, 72, 73, 84, 131

Eucharist, 34, 113-14, 116-18

    see also sacraments

fragmentation of the church, 21, 73-74, 76-80, 82, 84, 91-92

gospel, 10, 14-19, 55, 57, 59-65, 67-71, 92, 104, 107, 109-10

    false, 16, 34

Gregory, Brad, 80, 82, 84-85, 91

Henry VIII, 62-63

individualism, 73-74, 76, 78, 80-82, 84, 93, 110

kintsugi, 72, 140-41

Luther, Martin, 9, 23-24, 29, 34, 54-60, 69, 70, 75, 81, 109-10, 118

Lutheran tradition, 59, 69, 82, 102-3, 121

Methodist tradition, 8, 76, 103, 117

Nicene council

    see councils

Nicene Creed, 23, 29

orthodoxy, theological, 29, 30-32, 35

Peace of Westphalia, 82-83

Reformation, 9, 54, 69, 74-75, 103, 111-12, 116, 118

    English Reformation, 54, 61-62

    Protestant Reformation, 23, 33

reformed, 22, 32-33, 35-36

Reformed tradition, 32-33

Roman Catholic tradition, 6, 10, 20-21, 23-26, 28, 30, 33-34, 44-47, 49, 51, 53, 55-57, 61-64, 69- 72, 75-76, 80-82, 85, 87, 89, 92-93, 101, 103-4, 111-13, 118-20, 124, 126, 135

sacraments, 24, 29, 33, 34, 55, 109, 111, 116-8

    see also baptism; Eucharist

Sanneh, Lamin, 87-88, 91-92, 121

sin, 9, 13, 15-18, 33, 37, 39, 40-41, 43-45, 49, 50-51, 70, 104, 108, 118

sola gratia, 33, 86

sola scriptura, 33, 42

soteriology, 34-35, 131

triune God, 10, 11, 15, 36-38, 42-44, 69

unity of the church

    institutional, 21, 24, 27, 45, 49, 53, 61

    visible, 52-55, 60, 66

Zwingli, Ulrich, 59, 109-10

SCRIPTURE INDEX

Old Testament

Genesis
2:18, *75*
11:1, *122*
11:4, *122*
11:7, *122*
11:9, *122*

Isaiah
42:6, *75*
59:3-8, *38*

Micah
6:8, *18*

New Testament

Matthew
1:23-25, *14*
16:13-20, *126*
16:16, *57*
16:18, *57*
28:19, *53*

Mark
1:14-15, *15*
8:35, *17*
15:34-37, *14*

Luke
1:28, *136*
1:38, *136*
2:1-14, *138*
8:22-24, *14*

John
1:1, *13*

11:35, *14*
14:5-11, *13*
15:4-8, *66*
17, *77*
17:11, *77*
17:20-22, *78*
17:22, *13*
17:23, *78*
20:31, *13*

Acts
1:8, *18, 53*
2, *46*
2:4, *122*
2:6-11, *123*

Romans
1:1-6, *15*
1:16, *15*
3:23, *18*
6:3, *119*
6:5-6, *18*
6:8, *119*
8:9-11, *13*
8:17, *47*
12, *46*
15:16, *16*
15:20, *16*

1 Corinthians
1:18, *16*
3:4, *26*
3:6, *26*
12, *46*
12:12-14, *26*
13, *46*
13:12, *41*
15, *14*

15:3-8, *15*
15:49, *79*

2 Corinthians
3:17-18, *13*
4:7-9, *140*
4:16-18, *140*
5:17, *18*

Galatians
1:11, *16*
1:16, *16*

Ephesians
1:13, *16*
1:22-23, *46*
2, *126, 129*
2:8-9, *34*
2:12, *75, 130*
2:14, *84*
2:17-18, *131*
2:19, *75*
4:1-6, *119*
4:3, *77*
4:4-5, *77*
4:4-6, *27*
4:6, *77*
5, *46*

Philippians
1:27, *15*
2:6-8, *17*

Colossians
1:23, *15*

1 Timothy
2:5-6, *108*
3, *46*

2 Timothy
1:5, *133*
1:12, *134*
2:8, *15*
3:16, *132*
3:17, *134*

Hebrews
4:12, *42*

4:14-16, *14*
4:16, *35*
12:2, *79*

1 Peter
2:4-6, *110*
2:9, *110*
2:24, *18*

1 John
1:9, *18*
2:16, *17*
3, *47*

Revelation
7:9, *91*
19, *46*
21:4, *19*

AUTHOR'S PAGE

BETH
FELKER
JONES

at church blogmatics

FIND MORE FROM THE AUTHOR AT
BETHFELKERJONES.SUBSTACK.COM